The Barn

The Barn

A Vanishing Landmark in North America

Eric Arthur and Dudley Witney

A & W Visual Library

Library of Congress Catalog Card Number: 74-33776

ISBN 0-89104-004-8

Manufactured in the United States of America

Published by arrangement with New York
Graphic Society Ltd.

Designed by Paul Arthur + Associates Limited

The extract from *Far From the Madding
Crowd* by Thomas Hardy is reprinted by per-
mission of the Hardy Estate; Macmillan,
London and Basingstoke; and the Macmillan
Company of Canada Limited.

Dedication

We wish to honour the farmers and carpenter builders of the last three centuries in North America whose barns are represented in this book. With great traditions behind them in Europe, they nevertheless evolved a barn structure that was of their own time and place and dependent from thumb latch to ridge pole on the labour of their hands and the natural resources of forest and field.

With a high degree of imagination and a standard of craftsmanship not surpassed in the more sophisticated architecture of their own and our time, they built barns that can rank with the finest vernacular buildings of the world.

In honouring the forefathers who built the barns, we would not be neglectful of the present generation of farmers who have resisted the blandishments of salesmen who would alter the appearance of the barns beyond recognition.

The farmers are anonymous, but we can look back over several years to talks about the barn in situations as varied as sitting in a hospitable kitchen in winter or on a bale of hay in the mow in summer. To these, our unnamed collaborators, we wish to express our profound gratitude.

Eric Arthur.   *Dudley Witney*

Foreword

by Bill N. Lacy

Nearly all architectural histories of North America begin with the colonial brick houses that have survived to the present day; houses that connect with some European "school" in clear, orderly lines of continuity. On the other hand, hardly any self-respecting history of architecture ever devotes much space to our indigenous architecture. The architectural profession has always held rather rigid ideas about what can be legitimately considered architecture and what cannot. At one time, for example, industrial buildings were not acceptable, but the Bauhaus philosophy of functionalism changed all that. Now I suppose it is time for barns. And not a moment too soon either, for they are, in the popular environmental jargon, an "endangered species"–paradoxically in danger of disappearing for the very reasons that give them their significance: honest and unselfconscious design.

One wonders how barns and farm buildings could have been neglected by writers and historians for so long.

When man builds without giving any thought to "art" or toward creating something of beauty, when he builds to satisfy a well-stated function without frills, and when he is forced to build within narrow restrictions of materials and methods, the results, as with barns, are consistently the material of which museums are filled.

A hundred years ago, eighty-five out of every hundred persons in Canada and the United States lived on a farm. Today the same figures are true for those who live in cities. And at a time when seventy per cent of us are attempting, not very successfully, to live on two per cent of the land, a book about North American barns may be just the antidote we need to soothe our urban malaise. Indeed, this book is particularly timely inasmuch as the once lusty progenitor of the American barn, the family farm, has grown sick almost to death. Like those who attended quilting bees and baked homemade bread, the people who knew how to build barns have been consigned to oblivion. They are gone, and most of their splendid buildings soon will be.

It is the natural inclination of an architect, given barns to write about, to speak of their purity of line, of scale, of proportion and to extol their simple materials, simply chosen and artfully joined together. But barns are perfectly capable of speaking for themselves. Whether you are an architect, an art historian, or a fourth-grader, you have only to look at a Chester County stone barn in Pennsylvania to know it is a fine building. The same goes for a log connected barn in Quebec, one in frame on a mixed farm in Ontario, a circular barn in Vermont, or a Dutch barn in New York State. All are fine buildings, designed by men who didn't know they were designers–but who understood intuitively what kind of structure they needed.

To appreciate the significance of North American barns, the suburbanite in Shaker Heights or North Toronto must make a quantum psychological leap. Such a leap brings one to an extraordinary realization: the American who worked a family farm felt a much keener affinity for his barn than for his house and, indeed, the farmhouse was invariably a subordinate structure to the main barn.

One might try to explain the importance of the barn in strictly economic terms; certainly, the nineteenth-century man of the soil lived precariously enough to make sure that his most valuable possessions–his tools, his animals and their feed–were safely sheltered. But that doesn't account for a farmer's love for his barn. It doesn't account, for example, for the pride of a man named Cyrus Thompson in having the biggest barn in Haakon County, South Dakota–and his pleasure in filling it every Saturday night with fiddlers and square dancers until well into the twenties. Nor does it account for the self-denial of a farmer who, over the years, would spend thousands of dollars modernizing his dairy barn, but only recently felt he could afford to put indoor plumbing in his house.

A man's barn bespoke his worth as a man. It expressed his earthly aspirations and symbolized the substance of his legacy to his children.

If the barns that have existed for the last several hundred years in North America are now disappearing, we can at least take some consolation in the fact that their forms have begun to appear with noticeable regularity in contemporary architecture. The shed roof and other simple geometric shapes that characterize much of recent contemporary residential architecture are closely derivative of the barns and outbuildings of a passing era.

In assembling this tribute to the North American barn, Eric Arthur and Dudley Witney have not only done us the great service of preserving and passing along to us a rich architectural legacy, they have also dramatized a too-often forgotten fact: namely, that man naturally knows how to build good and true buildings.

Bill N. Lacy, AIA
Director, Architecture + Environmental Arts
National Endowment for the Arts
Washington, D.C.

Contents

a

a, b) A little-known indigenous architecture in western
Canada: the house of stucco over mud, with earth-
packed floor and heavy thatch as insulator for winter
as well as summer. The piggery, with its walls of
meshed sticks, could have an exact forebear in Iron-
Age Britain as a summer barn. The wall construction
will be recognized in later pages as cob or wattle and
daub (without the daub, which could be mud or plaster)
and is of very ancient origin.

Introduction

It is possible that millions now living in North America have never seen a barn, let alone been in one. In the foreseeable future, there is more than a possibility that, for many, the kind of barn illustrated in these pages will not be there to see. When one considers the exposure of our old barns to the winds of change, as well as those other winds that have buffeted them for a century or more, the marvel is that any are left for those who would try to comprehend the secrets that they hold.

It has been said of an older civilization:

"For at least four centuries before our own, changes which came to a farmstead and cottage were as gradual, as gentle, almost as imperceptible as the growth of a tree. Additions and renovations were carried out as need arose. Traditional methods were followed and the materials used were those which lay close at hand."[1]

Ours in North America is a briefer period, varying in regions from one to three hundred years, and can be looked back on for the same imperceptible growth, the same reliance on local well-tried materials from the soil or the forest, but no longer. In a lifetime, technology has been brought to bear on the barn as it has on the farm house, and this generation has witnessed the change on the old barns from roofs of thatch, of shingle, or of slate, the familiar and natural accompaniment to weathered pine, to metal. Hard, glossy and unsympathetic, the metal roof on an old barn is but a pointer that leads the farmer inevitably to a mail-order catalogue–a standardization of rural building, structure divorced from tradition and alien to the countryside.

Experience gained from this study would indicate that flexibility and readjustment to modern needs are not at all marked in the old barns. A great deal of space is taken up by the threshing floor, which recalls an operation all but extinct that goes back to ancient Egypt–the flailing and winnowing of wheat to separate the grain. It still has its use for the unloading of hay, but after that brief period it becomes a storehouse for penny farthing bicycles, mechanized equipment, and in the case of a surprising number of inland farmers, a boat–all anathema to the photographer. It is inevitable that some of our finest barns will soon become anachronisms. Many have already had their day and

c

b

c) The flail was a tool for threshing cereal crops: originating in biblical times, it was still in use in North America even in this century. A man in good health was able to give the sheaves thirty to forty strokes a minute, and his output for the day would average eight bushels of wheat, thirty of oats, eight of rye, or twenty of buckwheat.

a

Our concern is not with these modern "factories" but with old barns beloved of many, buildings that rank among the noblest works of man, and for the most part of anonymous man. Very rarely will the architect appear in these pages, because ours is the story of the master carpenter working with his crew to the point where the great framework of the barn lies ready for a multitude of men, fed and supported on the spot by their womenfolk, who in one long day will put the skeleton structure in position, their only tools being mallets, pike-poles, and levers. Nowhere is democracy and the brotherhood of man better demonstrated than by the barn raising bee.

In North America, the period of fine craftsmanship in panelling, staircases, and furniture, not to mention smaller artifacts like silver and glassware, was the eighteenth century. From then on, we, like other countries, were affected by the Industrial Revolution, which reached the climax of absurdity in England in the contents of the Crystal Palace of 1851 – itself, paradoxically, one of the finest buildings of the century, hardly yet excelled in the field of prefabrication by the products of modern technology. Domestic architecture in the farm houses of the continent was not adversely affected till late in the century, but it is to the barns of the last two hundred years that we go to see an unspoilt indigenous architecture where everything was wrought by human hands. House and barn were themselves the product of the land, and the quality pervading everything was one of homogeneity.

Everyone has experienced the pleasure, tactile as well as visual, of chairs, chests, and handrails that have been smoothed by thousands of loving hands and centuries of care. Fewer have enjoyed the same experience in the barn. Many a threshing floor has the polish of a ballroom floor from the old days of flailing wheat, and all the timbers within wagonload-height have taken on a honey colour, and all arrises have been softened, not by men's hands (though they have played a part), but by the rubbing of hay, straw and sheaves from harvests of a century or more.

How appropriate to that homogeneity seen in farm house, barn, and outbuildings is that purely North American artifact, the hand-split cedar snake fence, and how solid, even monumental, are the dry walls encircling

disappeared with little trace, or worse, still stand as partial ruins, "unwept, unhonoured and unsung."

The change over the centuries from the farm that was in itself both producer and consumer to the highly efficient operation which counted on trading for its survival was accentuated by population growth, the size and sprawl of cities, and, not a little in this century, by the demands put on it by two world wars. If we live in a period of crisis in farm management as in urban life, we live also in one of paradox and confusion. At the same time that the government of Prince Edward Island in Canada is bent on improving the economy of the island by eliminating the small farm through incorporation into larger holdings, we know of farms where proximity to lines of communication with urban centres is vastly more important than size, where cows stand on concrete floors and remain in their stalls during their lifetime, and others where hogs, turkeys and chickens by the ten thousands are fattened by their brief span on one fixed and narrow spot. Many a cow will never know the joy of winding "slowly o'er the lea."

a) Many a threshing floor acquired the polish of a ballroom floor in the old days of flailing wheat. This one is of pine, with oak pegs. Because of the treatment the boards got from the flailer, they were two inches and often more in thickness.

b

c

d

kitchens and ample bedrooms, all suitably furnished in their period. Few on seeing these restored cottages on a pleasant summer afternoon will realize what tales of killing work, and often of stark tragedy each dwelling could tell, especially the little one in log.

The story of the Pilgrim Fathers is told in the schools of the United States, just as in Canada the school boy learns of the settlement of Quebec in the sixteenth and seventeenth centuries. But real as these stories are in the history of our two countries, their distance in time makes them seem somehow less vivid today than the more recent record of pioneer farming in Ontario in the last century. As one writer put it, "the bone-shaking, heart-breaking, time-devouring roads of Canada run their torturous course through every book of travels and memoirs of the time."[2] These were the essential roads, and if they were heartbreaking, the labour was shared. It was not so for the settler who was shown his two hundred acre lot and left to his own resources in the depths of a primeval forest. Not the sunny forests he had known in Europe, "with their clear streams and bird songs and pools of wild flowers: it was a profoundly depressing place combining with the silence and solitude of the undersea, the sombreness and confinement of a cavern."[3]

The first thing was shelter. Giant pines and undergrowth had to be cleared before the first primitive shanty-dwelling could be made of poles with a roof of bark good enough to keep out the rain. Cooking was done over an open fire, and the settlers often ate from "slabs of wood and slept on hemlock boughs on the ground."[4]

The clearing of the forest went on, but the first cut trees were needed for the log cabin. Not infrequently, settlers from the old country brought little in the way of furniture with them and the stump of a local mammoth served as a table and smaller ones as stools. Strips of bark from the slippery elm stretched across a frame served as a bed.

"The winter would pass in clearing ground until the snow became too deep. This work would be varied by some hunting and fishing to add to the exiguous fare, and perhaps a long trip for more flour and pork to be got on credit from the store. The next summer, clearing and burning would go on again and the first wheat crop might be put in, sown broadcast among the stumps. Perhaps

fields. There are some that might without exaggeration be called cyclopean; now lichen-covered, they remain unshaken by all that nature in its fiercest winter moods has hurled against them. What stories they could tell of clearing the land before it was fit for tilling, of dragging great loads by oxen, and the eventual lifting in place by hand. The mind balks at the fact that, preceding the stacking of boulders to make boundary walls, the bush had to be cleared, and what fences were not of stone were formed by the gigantic octopus-like roots of pine trees – ten, twelve, even fifteen feet in diameter.

Taking precedence over all other urgent activities was the building of a shelter. Some pioneer cottages still exist, and are used on the farm for a variety of purposes. Even the city dweller can visit a "pioneer village" where enlightened communities have assembled examples of the house, the inn, the church, the general store, piggery and barn and sometimes more than one of each. For adult and child, nothing is likely to be appreciated so much as the pioneer log cabin, standing by itself or attached to the later and more commodious house with its parlour,

b) There is something majestic about the root fence, and equally splendid were the monarchs that they once fed and supported in the primeval forest. Location: Vasey, Ontario.

c) Unlike the fence in Australia which keeps out rabbits, this snake fence (really a straight rail) is no deterrent to snakes. It is rare to find one where the toprail takes on the shape of a reptile's head. Most rails are cedar, but an old friend could remember walnut being used on his grandfather's farm in the 1850's.

d) Not the earliest type of "boulder lifter," but a handsome and efficient piece of equipment that anticipated the heavy machines of modern times.

a

b

twenty bushels to the acre would be gathered and this, if it could be sold, was the first money crop. More often it had to be eaten.

"The crop was cut with a sickle, gathered into the house, onto the beaten ground before the house, and threshed with a flail. The settler would then load a sackful on his shoulder and walk perhaps twenty miles or more through the woods to a mill. In the fall, he might make this trip three or four times to be sure of having enough flour in the house. Those who were not within reach of a mill ground the grain themselves; some used a coffee mill which they had been advised to bring with them. It took a day to grind a day's consumption. Others pounded the wheat in the hollow stump of a tree and ate it in sourdough cakes, bran and all. Some were at times reduced to chewing the grains until they were softened enough to make porridge. This gruel and a glass of whiskey was often the breakfast of parents and children alike through a long winter. Pork boiled or fried and hard cakes of dough were the other meals. It was either work without end, or the elementary life of the hunter with its bare subsistence for the family. Either way, only the toughest survived."[5] The barn and the comforts of a settled community were some way off.

That was a pioneering story in the Ontario of the 1830's, and earlier experiences can hardly have been happier. Many a traveller in the eighteenth century commented on houses and barns that he saw, and, while to the south of the border things were more settled than they were in Ontario, it is interesting to learn from the records of the State of Pennsylvania in 1798, that that state "was then overwhelmingly of log or cabin barns."

These eighteenth-century visitors from Europe were fascinated by the barns they saw in their travels in the New World, and, fortunately for us, they kept diaries which frequently found a home in print. They were equally attracted by the farmer's house, and their description of both the buildings and the people whose hospitality they enjoyed make interesting and often moving reading for those who can follow them on the journey a hundred or two hundred years later. Some arrived at a time when the barn could be described as big as "pallaces," and the house, by comparison, diminutive and cramped. On enquiry, the farmer would tell his visitor that

a) These pictures represent three stages in the life of a Canadian farmer. The first is the shanty in a clearing in the forest.

b) Fifteen years later, a barn has been added, and a house of hewn logs.

c

d

best of the barns, flour mills, bridges, and houses of Ontario and Quebec seemed even more pressing at the same time that reading and visiting indicated the continuity of the historic lines of communication between Canada and the neighbouring states of Pennsylvania, New York, and Vermont.

One of the best known barn types in Ontario is still called a Pennsylvania barn, and on the North Shore of the St. Lawrence River there is the "Schoharie" barn, acclimatized to life in Canada, and blood brother to the Dutch barn in the state of New York. The language and customs of many of the people of central rural Ontario are identical with those of their fellow sectarians in the United States, though they have been separated geographically for well over a hundred years. As far back as 1834 in Toronto, a writer in the *Toronto Pocket Manual for Travellers* speaks of "a singular sect in this vicinity of whom you occasionally see a specimen in Town. They are called Tunkers and Dunkards." Another goes so far as to say that "Canadians from the neighbourhood of Kitchener (formerly Berlin) are as Dutch as the Dutch from Lancaster and Lebanon."[7]

Before embarking on a study of the barn in North America, one naturally looks to the literature on the barn, and, for what one might find, to the barn in literature. Of the latter, Thomas Hardy would seem the most likely novelist to make use of it for one of his Wessex tales, and he was, after all, an architect until thirty years of age. Nowhere in the landscape he loved was there anything more indigenous or more characteristic than the barn, and he doesn't disappoint us. In *Far from the Madding Crowd* he writes of Bathsheba Eversdene's barn: "They sheared in the great barn, called for the nonce the Shearing-barn, which on ground-plan resembled a church with transepts. It not only emulated the form of the neighbouring church of the parish, but vied with it in antiquity. Whether the barn had ever formed one of a group of conventual buildings nobody seemed to be aware: no trace of any such surroundings remained. The vast porches at the sides, lofty enough to admit a waggon laden to its highest with corn in the sheaf, were spanned by heavy-pointed arches of stone, broadly and boldly cut, whose very simplicity was the origin of a grandeur not apparent in erections where more ornament has been attempted.

after seven harvests, some said nine, a proper house would be built.

Often too late to save the finest barns, societies like the British and Scottish National Trusts and Heritage Trusts in Ontario and Nova Scotia have sprung up with the sole object of preserving what is best in what is left of their countries' architectural treasures. In some areas of North America, recording has been done on a magnificent scale,[6] but preservation lags lamentably behind–even for the house. The architectural claims for the barn are known only to a few, and those who are knowledgable on the subject must have become familiar with the question, "Did you say you were making a study of barns? You mean barns-BARNS?"

An interest in barns goes back for this writer at least fifty years when, as a student, he was as moved by the timeless beauty of the smallest of medieval English barns as he was awed by the nobility of the interiors of the great tithe barns that dominated the ecclesiastical community prior to the dissolution of the monasteries under Henry VIII. Over the years, in a new country, the urgency of the need to record, or even better to preserve the

c) Thirty years after settlement, everything is transformed–the house is commodious, barns are ample, and the forest is reduced to a woodlot.

d) Early travellers in North America commented in their diaries on the almost monumental scale of the barn in relation to the diminutive log cabin of the farmer and his family. The modern traveller cannot help but be equally impressed by the comparison, since several, in use or abandoned, still can be seen.

a

The dusky, filmed, chestnut roof, braced and tied in by huge collars, curves, and diagonals, was far nobler in design, because more wealthy in material, than nine-tenths of those in our modern churches. Along each wall was a range of striding buttresses, throwing deep shadows on the spaces between them, which were perforated by lancet openings, combining in the proportions the precise requirements both of beauty and ventilation.

"One could say about this barn, what could hardly be said of either the church or the castle, akin to it in age and style, that the purpose which had dictated its original erection was the same with that to which it was still applied. Unlike and superior to either of those two typical remnants of medievalism, the old barn embodied practices which had suffered no mutilation at the hands of time. Here at least the spirit of the ancient builders was at one with the spirit of the modern beholder. Standing before this abraded pile, the eye regarded its present usage, the mind dwelt upon its past history, with a satisfying sense of functional continuity throughout – a feeling almost of gratitude, and quite of pride, at the permanence of the idea which had heaped it up....

"Today the large side doors were thrown open towards the sun to admit a bountiful light to the immediate spot of the shearers' operations, which was the wood threshing-floor in the centre, formed of thick oak, black with age and polished by the beating of flails for many generations, till it had grown as slippery and as rich in hue as the state-room floors of an Elizabethan mansion."

Having reread these quotations from Hardy, one went with expectation of further literary sources to that usually reliable reservoir of information on a wide variety of topics, the *Oxford Dictionary of Quotations*, only to find the barn exhausted as a subject by three not very helpful quotations of which one will suffice:

> *He'll sit in a barn*
> *And to keep himself warm*
> *Will hide his head under his wing*
> *Poor thing.*

Even more discouraging is the eleventh edition of the *Encyclopaedia Britannica* which is usually regarded by scholars as an invaluable source of information on the humanities and on artifacts of all kinds. On the subject of barns, it is silent.[8]

a) The interior of the barn at Great Coxwell, demonstrating very clearly the church arrangement of the nave and aisles. The barn measured 152' x 44' by 48' to the ridge.

b) A thatched barn in Charlevoix County, Quebec. Few remain in eastern Canada, and the itinerant thatcher no longer plies his craft.

b

c

Half a dozen dictionaries would throw light on the derivation of the word "barn," and the Oxford Dictionary's "covered building for storing grain and in winter usage of hay, straw, flax and other produce of the earth" may be regarded as typical. It will be noticed that in that brief statement there is no reference to horses or cattle, for a very good reason that will be discussed later, and grain as seeds of wheat, oats, barley or rye would take up a very small space in the barn compared with fodder. The place for the storage of grain is the granary, which might

c) Unsurpassed among the barns of the world is the medieval tithe barn at Great Coxwell in Berkshire, England. Externally, it takes the form of a church and, internally, of a nave and aisles. This plan form goes back two millennia in Europe, and has come to be known by architectural historians as basilican. It is to be seen in barns as geographically remote from each other as Great Coxwell in the United Kingdom, New York State, and the environs of Toronto.

be in the barn, as it usually was in North America, or in a separate building. Grain still in the ear or the sheaf waiting to be threshed might fit the dictionary meaning.

However, to continue with the dictionary, the word "barn" comes from the Old English *bere* meaning barley and *ern* a place or closet, hence, a barley place. Barley was the principal crop in early times, and supplied as well the standard measure of three barley corns to an inch.[9]

In this chapter and elsewhere, reference will be made at times to a building closely identified with the barn and almost universally part of it, but not often found by name in American writing: the *byre*.[10] The byre always was, and is, a cow house, and that was its Old English meaning. If the Oxford Dictionary is curt in its reference to barns including "derog. an unadorned building," it unbends on the byre, going so far as to include the familiar Scottish phrase "to muck the byre," meaning to "cleanse," and to quote Wordsworth in 1805, "Long ere heat of noon from byre or field the kine were brought." The interested reader may go further and look for the verses in an old Scottish song "The Muckin' o' Geordie's byre." The point about the barn and byre as separate buildings with strictly different functions is that they may still be found among ethnic groups of European origin in North America, and that the words and buildings are in common use in places as removed from each other as eastern Canada and New Zealand. In Britain they have had their different uses since Saxon times. In Ontario in the 1830's, we read of Lou, "who would tuck up the train of her dress, put her milk pail over her arm and set off for the stable, saying she saw no reason why she could not milk as well in a satin gown as in her highland byrewoman's dress."[11]

The byre, in Lou's case, could have been a separate building, or, as in the Pennsylvania and many other barn types, it would occupy the lower floor. Occasionally, those inappropriate terms "cow house" and "cow shed" may creep into these pages. Both suggest a building of shaky construction, separate from the barn – but how incongruous, how absurd to use the word "shed" for the cow department in the great Shaker barn at Hancock! It is a byre with two millennia of tradition behind its name.

In Britain and the continent of Europe, books written about barns or house and barn are of this or the last century, except for the diaries of observant, intelligent early travellers. Contemporary literature in English dealing exclusively with the barn in North America is extremely limited, but three books have been of great value as research material. All are from the United States, one, broad in its coverage[12] and two limited to a particular barn type in a particular state[13]. In Canada, generally, nothing has been published, but one book in French has saved many an historic barn from oblivion and provided a storehouse of material that has proved invaluable in a study of the barn in Quebec.[14] The state of Pennsylvania sets a high standard in the cultivation of an interest in local folklore, and in the publication of excellent magazines containing scholarly articles on a wide variety of artifacts with the barn in an honoured place.

By contrast with North America, the people of the Netherlands have declared their oldest and finest barns to be national monuments, and a dozen or more splendid books record the barns of the country by photograph, measured drawings, and text. The same is true of the Swiss, whose great house/barns are represented in a number of beautifully illustrated books. In Britain and elsewhere on the continent of Europe similar recording is done by architectural historians, but of even greater significance is the importance attached to the preservation and restoration of those buildings designated by government as national monuments and as proud examples of a people's culture and heritage. Along with the great cathedrals, castles, and manor houses, one will always find the barn.

Perhaps because of the inaccessibility of the literature on the North American barn, one becomes aware of the difference between public concern for the preservation of old houses of architectural merit and barns of the same period. Interest in the houses is widespread and still growing; many cities and states publish brochures telling citizens and visitors where such houses are to be found, something of their history and why they are considered important. Adults' and children's tours are now commonplace, and for the latter, a place is found in many progressive school curricula.

a

a) A splendid little granary in Galica in Northern Spain. Called *horreos*, these granaries are obviously a source of family or village pride in proportion to their size. The cross suggests the blessings of the church, and the flaired cap to the stone supports an obstacle for the rats to hurdle.

Is it possible that enthusiasm for the historic house is partly due to the knowledge the layman has acquired, and that his enjoyment comes from putting it to use–especially when he is successful in finding something not well known or, at any rate, unlisted? For the reasonably well informed layman, the house has few secrets, while the barn has many and they are not easily disclosed. They are, however, every bit as romantic and venerable, with roots going back to a remote past in Great Britain and the continent of Europe. By contrast, the architectural story of the house, which will likely be roughly contemporary with the barn in the farm complex, is comparatively easy to trace. In the old areas covered by this study, the house will in all likelihood, except in Quebec, be Georgian or colonial in design, or some variation of Gothic made popular by the romantic movement of the late eighteenth and early nineteenth century. If colonial, the lay enthusiast will recognize details that had their origin in Georgian England and the renaissance of classic architecture in Europe. He will recognize the Doric or Ionic orders, whether Greek or Roman in the porch; each

element in the cornice has a Latin name known to the older carpenter and tinsmith, and the gentle slope of the roof recalls its origin in the sunny tiled roofs of Italy.

The farm house of Gothic design presents no great problem in identification, even if it is partially obscured by "gingerbread" in cornices, gable, barge boards, or any other part of the building where such playful medieval conceits would please the nineteenth-century farmer's wife. The telltale elements of pointed mullioned windows, label moulds, bosses, and a steeper roof are there for the least discriminating layman to see, and their prototype in the middle ages in Europe will be apparent.

The barn offers no such traditional clues, nor do any of its external features take us back to those elements in the colonial house that had their origin in Greece in the fifth century B.C., or the Rome of Caesar Augustus. Part of the charm and definitely part of the mystery surrounding the origins of the barn in North America are that it is indigenous, it is part of a vernacular culture, and its authors are anonymous. American scholars may have found more, but in the research for this book only two barns designed by architects were found, and only one complete specification, which was handwritten. The more important of the two is interesting because, although its reputed architect was a distinguished Polish engineer, Col. Sir Casimir Nicholas Stanislas Gzowski, and, at the time, a recent immigrant to Canada, the barn he designed shows no features in plan or section and few in elevation dissimilar to the anonymous stone barns in the district. History, custom, and climate have been powerful factors in the evolution of our barns. The searcher will look in his travels, not for classic columns, cymas recta or resersa, cavettos, dentils and the rest, but rather for things at first sight mundane: the cantilevered mow, the location of the wagon doors, the height of the eaves, the size of boards, the many secrets hidden in the timber framing, and the pitch, shape and material of roofs–all of which will tell a story. He is bound to get a thrill on discovering exotic forms like the circle and the octagon, and he will be surprised to find that, in Canada, a number of houses and barns are still thatched.

b) Shafts of light from seen and unseen sources, and the warm glow of sunshine on time-worn timbers. The reader remembering such a barn will recall the acrobatic display of the swallows and the echoing beating of pigeons' wings.

b

a

b

Usually, he will get a good reception from the farmer and his wife. Relief on her part will come from the fact that, unlike previous visitors, he has expressed no desire to explore the house; cameras, note books, and the casual mention of an interest in the history and the aesthetics of the barn, will rid her of any suspicion that she is addressing representatives of a mortgage company or shrewd real estate operators. That barrier hurdled, the farmer himself will recover from the shock of meeting a barn lover, even though his experience has not always been the best with such intruders as salesmen or hunters. He will soon enter into the spirit of the visit, and information will soon flow on the history of the barn and its construction going back several generations, and barns in a radius of several miles that "mustn't be missed" will be located on the map.

The barn seeker knows the joy that can be got from his hobby, and how patient he must be in its pursuit. The multi-lane highway is not for him, and lesser highways carved out of the countryside will profit him little. It is on the byways and lanes that he will know the thrill of the prospector finding gold. Like the prospector, he will have his off days, but the sights and smells of the countryside will be reward enough. And then will come a day when he will find a barn, or even two, of a type he has not seen before, and he will experience the thrill of the prospector, the fisherman, and the bird watcher all in one. If the barn exterior gives him pleasure, what he sees within will be no less rewarding. Whether it be a first or a tenth sight of the same interior, he will experience the kind of feeling the visitor gets standing in the nave of a cathedral like St. Paul's in London. He will be immediately conscious of space, the space provided by the lofty nave and flanking lower aisles, of shafts of light from seen and unseen sources, and, in the barn, of the warm glow on time-worn timbers. Part of the picture he will take away with him will be of an aerial acrobatic display by the swallows and the echoing beating of pigeons' wings.

It is true that south of the border many historic barns have been recorded, but even in Pennsylvania there is no inventory of old barns, and excitement runs high when an unlisted splendid specimen appears unexpectedly through a gap in a hedgerow. From the beginning, this study has had as a guiding

a) As interesting as the finest single great barn is the grouping of modest buildings in close proximity to the farmer's house. This example tells the story, not only of the seemingly casual planning of house and buildings, but of the homogeneity of material—here seen in chinked logs, vertical planking, and cedar shingles.
Location: village of Schutt, Ontario.

b) Beautiful to the traveller in the countryside are fields of fireweed or mustard, but their beauty is understandably lost on the farmer.

c) Silos in the new landscape.
Location: near Washington, Ontario.

c

d

principle the barn as architecture, rather than as a subject for antiquarian research. Consequently, we have not neglected the exotic barns of the second half of the nineteenth century which, not fitting into a well documented tradition in the area, would be ignored by the historian in a specialized field. Of barns in this category, it is hoped that some of the circular barns in Quebec and Vermont will justify the decision to search for beauty and design quite regardless of age. Always to be borne in mind is the ephemeral nature of so many of the things to be enjoyed in the countryside of North America if the time is taken – things like covered bridges, wayside shrines, outside bake ovens, and barns which a posterity nearer than we think will know only through the pages of a book.

This introduction should not close without a word on the barns that, in the last few decades, have made so great a change in the landscape of rural North America. Our old barns fade into insignificance against the scale and glitter of modern steel and concrete structures in which a revolution has taken place in the storage of corn and the feeding and care of cattle. Most striking are the silos, which now dominate a skyscape once memorable for its dreaming spires.

The farmer owner of these establishments has become an industrialist: he may even be a corporation – a far cry from the "progressive" farmer of not so long ago who saw himself in a brave new world as the initiator of a measure of hygiene, automatic milking and soothing music for his cows.

We accept these new farm buildings as we must accept the inevitable, but we look forward to their evolution in matters of design and material to the point where a comparison may be made with the barns of an earlier era, in which beauty and a surprising degree of efficiency emerged as a solution to the basic problem of feeding, storage and shelter.

d) "All the timbers within a wagon load height have taken on a honey colour, and all have been softened, not by men's hands, though they have played a part, but by the rubbing of hay, straw and sheaves from harvests of a century or more."

e) Cyclopean and often lichen-covered are the dry walls encircling fields. The stones were hauled by oxen and levered into place by human hands and primitive equipment.
Location: Vasey, Ontario.

e

Part 1

The Barn

Where I behold the farmer's early care/In the revolving labours of the year.
John Gay, Rural Sports

MY BARN *by Dean Hughes*

Look there!
   It stands today
As strong as six-score memoried years ago;
A big barn built to hold fat crops in its massive mows,
As provender to last the long rows of sleek cows,
In the stables underneath,
The long dark winter through.
      Examine, if you will,
These giant plates and beams,
These stalwart loins and limbs and thighs.
Each one was once upon a splendid time
A giant pine
Singing a hundred feet towards the skies,
Then topped to sixty feet of needed length,
Hewed from the round to fourteen inches square.
       See there!

The marks of hewing axe and adze,
Swung straight and true.
     Read there the tale
Of toil and sweat and a fine pride
In shaping these great timbers.
      Stand with me
A wondrous moment.
     In that crafted tree
Is history enough of old great-grandsire times
A century ago and more.
      Those sheathing boards,
Those tenons, mortices and dowels,
Those thews and sinews,
Those mitres bevelled true,
Fitted in tight embrace to fight the winds
And the strong side-thrust of the sheaves and hay.
There stands my barn!
     Monument to the past!
      Feast for the present!
       Song for the future!

Now fades the glimmering landscape on the sight,
And all the air a solemn stillness holds
Save where the beetle wheels his droning flight,
And drowsy tinklings lull the distant folds.
Thomas Gray, Elegy Written in a Country Churchyard

You put the barn good and far from the house in
case it burned; like the night they woke up in a strange light
and it was the glare of barn-flame in the bureau mirror: everything
gone.

But at the home farm the three barns were still
there, an (open) square standing for any child to wander in. Quiet
and muffled in winter, the sound of the bull bashing impenitently
against his stake and his wall; animal bodies bumping and squealing
and rubbing; pock-pock-squawk from the henhouse, fierce indignant
broody hens warming china eggs.

The air was floury at feed-time. You could sit [when
you were alone] on the edge of the calves' pen letting the calves
lick your bare knees as you felt their starred foreheads: cow-lick.
You could sit in the buckwheat as if you were in hot-sand, pouring
the smooth dark grain down your legs and wondering if there
was a word for the rounded double-prism shape. Or watch old Molly
the blind horse bringing load after load of straw in between
the lofts after threshing; or was it hay after haying? Would a
city child know?

The guineas stayed in the trees, but the banty hens
played in the stable behind the horses' hooves, where no child
went; and in the doorway, cats suckled whatever kittens came
along. In the cowbarn, Ab put mangles through the mangle.

But the sheds fell down on the democrats and cutters;
no stone-boats drew the milk-cans to the road; the families ran
to girls and city-fellers; the hired men went away; and we were

left with the stories.

Marian Engel

Nothing remains so vivid in the mind of man as childhood memories of the barn—of cows and horses and, listening in the mow to the hooting of the owl, the acrobatic display of swallows, and the echoing beating of pigeons' wings.

William Roberts THE BRUSO BARN

For generations the barn has been beloved of artists who see in its simple form and the muted grey of pine or red or yellow boards something calling irresistibly for perpetuation in paint.

Even for the entrepreneur, there must linger nostalgic memories of the barn as a place of adventure and fun—memories that he hopes will be evoked in the minds of the patrons of his restaurant or dance hall. Hence the lure of the Red Barn.

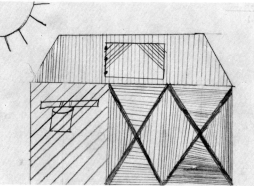

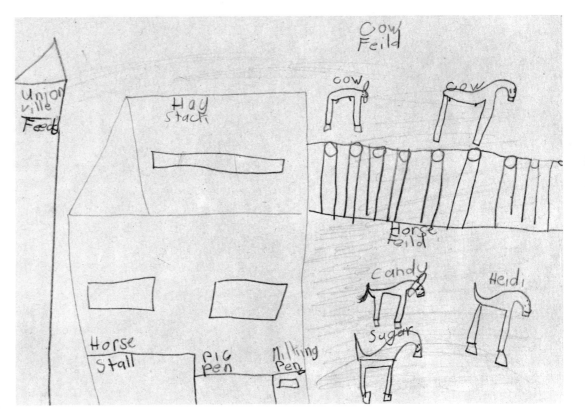

This is the farmer sowing his corn/That kept the cock that crowed in the morn/That waked the priest all shaven and shorn/That married the man all tattered and torn/That kissed the maiden all forlorn/That milked the cow with the crumpled horn/That tossed the dog/That worried the cat/That killed the rat/That ate the malt/That lay in the house that Jack built. Nursery Rhyme

There is nothing so appalling, so awesome as a burning barn,
unless it be a burning ship at sea.

Part 2

The Barn in North America

"Let every structure needful for a farm arise in castle semblance."
Sanderson Miller, an amateur eighteenth-century architect, quoted by Sir Kenneth Clark.
The stable barn at Maitland, Ontario, was built prior to 1840 by a retired Hudson's Bay factor. The house and attached stone outbuildings across the road are just as fine as the battlemented wall to the barnyard.

Interior showing the framework of a barn in
Schoharie, New York.

The Dutch Barn

Chapter 1

We are about to look at a type of barn that is among the oldest in North America. It is found particularly in New York State on lands bordering the Hudson, Scoharie, and Mohawk Rivers, which were settled by Dutch immigrants in the seventeenth and eighteenth centuries, but also in New Jersey. It is known in New York State as the Dutch barn, and one of its unique features is that the wagon doors are placed at each end of the barn, and not on the side like all other barn types in North America.

One would naturally ask why so radical a change was introduced by the Dutch. Was it the result of a whim of an influential member of the community, or did it have its roots in a tradition of farm building in the Old World? We shall find it to be the latter, for its roots go very deep indeed: in fact, to the kind of farmstead that had its origin in the dim reaches of European history, and to an internal arrangement of spaces that anticipated the plan form of the great Christian cathedrals.

The Dutch barn of the Netherlands has two points of visual affinity with the church: the end entrance, and a plan based on nave and aisles which, in the barn, serve as threshing floor and cattle stalls.[1] It could be argued that the ecclesiastical parallel is weakened by the fact that in the church there are no doors at the east end to match those at the west, but in the Saxon and Netherlands barns, the prototypes of those found in New York State, a single entrance was usual and side entrances uncommon.

Although the New York State barn shares this ancient lineage, it is quite unpretentious when seen in its setting: a modest, strangely proportioned building, somewhat wider than it is long, and clapboarded. It is "end drive" because it did not make sense for the wagon

to be backed out in the direction whence it came, to be turned about in the restricted space of a threshing floor, or right or left through side doors. If in threshing time a through draft could be counted on, both sets of doors could be opened and the sheaves flailed on the floor and winnowed in the wind to separate the grain from the chaff.

The plan of these Dutch North American barns has come to be called "basilican" by historians, and the term is obviously apt. It came about, perhaps as long ago as two millennia, to meet the requirements of a central wide space for threshing that was convenient to narrower spaces for cattle and horses, and a simple structural system in timber that would support the roof and a snow load, as well as whatever was stored as fodder over the threshing floor. There might have been other ways of handling the former, but, as the animals faced into the nave from which they were fed, it was a functional and very practical solution.

The traditional pattern in the architecture of the church was a separation of nave from aisles by means of columns spaced at regular intervals forming bays. Columns could be marble or stone, but in the barn they were wood. The analogy would be complete except that the soaring nave is not found in the Dutch barn. It is there and seen with difficulty in the summer when the mow is empty, and visible through a low ceiling formed by poles which support the fodder required by the cattle in winter.

The history of the barn is a long one, going back to prototypes in iron-age Britain, when the barn took the form of an upturned ship. This was the barn of the fourth century B.C. It was rectangular and was formed by "crucks," or the meeting of a pair of tree trunks roughly trimmed of their branches, and so bent by nature that, when brought together, they formed a curved A. With one pair of crucks at the end of the structure, and another at the other, the two were braced by a ridgepole. The walls, which were curved, were filled with a network of wattle sticks and covered with mud or plaster: the prototype of walling used in the seventeenth century in the barns of Quebec. When the cruck barn is looked at upside down, it takes the shape of a ship.

Is it a coincidence that this ancient architectural form, echoed in the vaulting of the

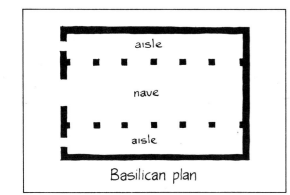

Basilican plan

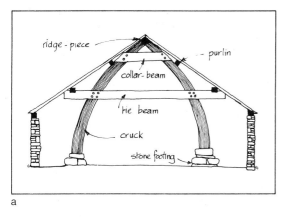

a

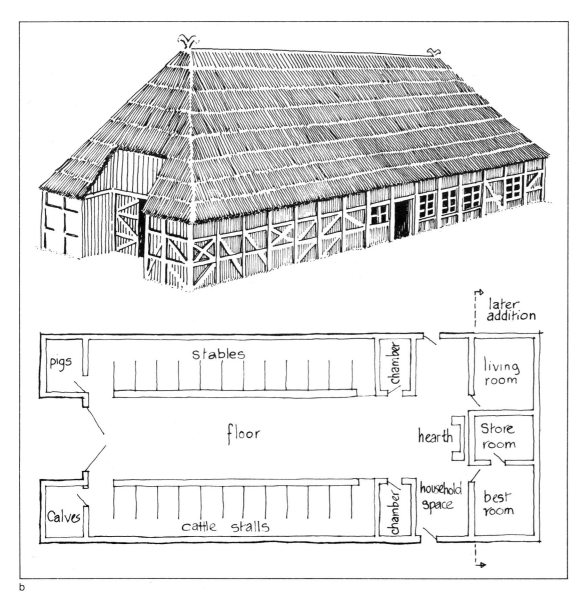

b

Gothic cathedral, fits so perfectly the derivation of the word "nave," which we get from the Latin *navis*, a ship? The German word for nave is *schiff*, or ship.

Before looking at New World barns, it is interesting to recall the historic barns that even today stand on the home soil of the emigrants. They brought with them ways of farming and skills in building handed down from father to son over countless generations, and it will be seen how old traditions of the fine craftsmanship persisted in spite of the pioneer problems of mere existence in a land as yet untamed.

From time immemorial, Europeans have lived in close contact with their animals, and farmsteads still exist that combine under one roof barn, byre, and house. The Saxon house/farm in Europe is said to have been a "survival of the ancient and typically Saxon house common to all Aryan peoples at an early stage in their development."[2] In the sketch, the basilican division into nave and aisles is seen in undeniable form, but its mirror-like symmetry is not at all what one would expect of a primitive people. Symmetry, inevitably, involves drawing and cannot be achieved by oral information or the wave of a hand. Amazingly, such farmsteads are still to be found in Saxony and the Netherlands, though less symmetrical, and many illustrated here have been restored and maintained by a wise and generous government which, quite properly, regards ancient barns as landmarks in the cultural evolution of its country.

This very early farmstead was rectangular and steep roofed; hipped at both ends, and entered at one end through double doors. The sight within would be truly amazing, particularly if night could be assumed and the countryside quiet under deep snow, because this was the home of a farmer and his family as well as a barn. The large central space or threshold[3] would be occupied by men and maidservants enjoying each others' company in games or conversation, but they would be seen only in an almost impenetrable gloom illuminated by the glow from a peat fire, never extinguished, which burned on a low hearth at the far end of the room. The threshing floor must have been furnished with rugged benches and tables, and one can imagine the desire on someone's part to cry with Shakespeare's Capulet, "A hall, a hall,

a) The cruck was a very ancient framing system in which a pair of tree trunks roughly trimmed of their branches were so bent by nature that when brought together they formed a curved A. Two pairs of crucks braced by a ridge pole formed the frame.

b) The very ancient plan form of the Saxon house, in which the family lived in the same space and under the same roof as the animals. The family enjoyed restricted quarters by the hearth; threshing took place in the central space or nave, which was flanked by cows on

give room and foot it girls, more light ye knaves and turn the tables up." But this was not a medieval hall – a hall it is true, but one never free from combustible materials, and there would be no lamps. The proverb is still remembered in rural England: "a lantern on the table is death in the stable."[4] For ordinary use or emergency, water was available from a well near the hearth.

Through the murk, a glimpse could be had of the family gathered about the fire at the end of the room, but most surprising would be the sight of cows on the left and horses on the right facing into the 'nave' from which they were fed. When time came to retire, probably announced by the patriarch farmer himself, the women mounted a ladder to their sleeping quarters over the cows and the men over the horses. The patriarch can be imagined seated at the far end of the room surrounded by his family. About him is a limited space with doors to the outside and windows, not yet glazed, but no doubt covered with a semi-transparent parchment made from sheep skin. Beds are but wall beds set in cupboards behind the hearth. An English writer mentions buildings in the north of England where the family, servants and animals dwelt under a common roof, but not in such close proximity as the inmates of the Saxon house just visited. Even so, "they were not so farre distant in sunder that the goodman being in his bed may lightlie hear what is done in each of them with ease, and call quickly to his meinie [household] if any danger should attack him."[5]

Writing in 1898, Mr. Addy could say that there were persons still living in England who remember how farmers' menservants were required to sleep in a gallery or hay loft over the cattle. Of conditions in England, Wales, Ireland, Germany, and Scandinavia in 1678, he says that the custom was not uncommon for the entire family including servants to sleep in one room and "when night came, straw, dried rushes, heath or dried ferns were spread upon the floor; and those unprovided with beds or couches laid themselves down, each under the bench or table upon which he or she sat."[6]

The wall with the wall beds once represented the end of the house, but after many centuries of discomfort, rooms were added as shown on the sketch plan; a step toward the final (but not universal) separation of women from the barn, and eventually, of male and female farm hands. Prior to this addition, a small but enormous step in the journey toward a civilized way of living, life in this home-cum-byre-cum-barn must have been almost intolerable for serf, master, mistress and her children. The invention of the chimney was at least a thousand years off, and its feeble predecessor, a mere hole in the roof, was dependent on the vagaries of the wind. There would be a time in the evolution of the farmstead when a small smoke house would be built for the smoking of meat, but in the Saxon house the whole interior, in addition to its many other functions, was a smoke house and hams, bacon, and meat of all kinds hung from the ceiling over the threshing floor. The reader will recall the light at night not from flaming logs, but from the glow of burning peat, a light that was less by a great deal than is enjoyed in a modern cocktail bar. He cannot help but think of the smoke, the lowing of cattle and the squealing of pigs, and what various writers on the period have called the "stench." That may have been something to which, over a period of time, one became accustomed, or even (as one learns in a recent book about a member of the house of Krupp in Germany who had smells from his stables piped into his bedroom) something to be relished.

Thanks to the enlightened policy of the Netherlands government, a number of historic barns have been moved and rebuilt in an open air museum in a beautiful park at Arnhem. Illustrations show how skilfully these barns have been rehabilitated, even to their interiors and the furniture and colourful bric-a-brac that the farmer and his wife once enjoyed. These barns are important to us because they, or barns like them, were the ones that the emigrants knew when they left Holland for the New World.

Among the oldest are the Loshoes type, of which the one from Lichtenvoorde has much in common with the ancient Saterland barn. It is basilican in plan, and one can look from the wagon entrance through the threshing floor to the ever-burning fire. On entering, two rooms for pigs are passed on the right and a sunken room for cattle on the left. Research has not unearthed other barn types in Europe or elsewhere where the cattle stall floors were depressed, but the custom born of centuries was continued in New York State.

one side with women's quarters above and horses on the other with menservants above. Very important in a study of the Dutch barn and its evolution in Europe and later in New York State is the position of the wagon doors at the end of the threshing floor. This became, over the centuries, the distinctive feature of the Dutch barn. It is not found in any other barn types in North America.

1. pigyard 1a. pigsty 2. sunken stall.
3. threshing floor 4. weaving room 5. cupboard
6. cupboard-bed 7. bedroom 8. living-room
& kitchen with fireplace 9. wash-kitchen 10. bedroom

b

On the right is a weaving room with an indication of two looms facing a better than usual bedroom separated from the "wash kitchen" by a cupboard bed. The phrase "wash kitchen" may be what it actually says, and cooking was still done over the fire which is indicated by a circle. The photograph of the interior shows that the cobbled floor of the family area surrounding the hearth stops abruptly on a line beyond which is the earth-packed smooth threshing floor. Over all was the pole ceiling supporting the hay.

Loshoes Zeijen resembles Lichtenvoorde in several ways, but in more gracious days it has been extended to include the "best" room with three bed cupboards taking up one wall. One whole aisle (3) is used for cattle, and it faces 4 and 5, one of which is for sheep and the other for calves. In the oldest plans available for study, the room flanking the entrance was invariably devoted to pigs, less a position of honour than the result of a desire to keep them as remote as possible from the "hearth place."

During the restoration and reconstruction of Zeijen, photographs were taken of construction, and they are of considerable

a) This is one of two barns of a type known in the Netherlands as "Loshoes." They have been moved, set up, and marvellously restored in the museum park at Arnhem. This barn is from Lichtenvoorde in lush grass cattle country. The illustration suggests a sunny and habitable home with no indication of the presence of cattle and pigs under the same roof.

b) The plan with its legend requires no explanation, but the reader might imagine himself at the entrance and see, if it is night, the glowing ever-burning peat fire at the far end of the threshing floor. Two bedrooms and a weaving room indicate an improvement over the Saxon house.

c) One has only to look at the barn from Zeijen to "feel that centuries of experience and tradition, of weather in all its moods: of the needs of cattle and the simple comforts of the family have gone into its design.... Externally, one could regard it as the equal of any of the vernacular monuments of the world. It is an organic thing, part and parcel of the earth."

d

e

f

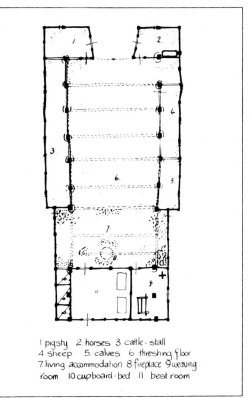

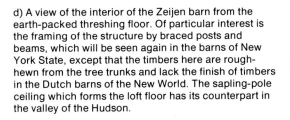
1. pigsty 2. horses 3. cattle-stall
4. sheep   5. calves   6. threshing floor
7. living accommodation 8. fireplace 9. weaving
room 10. cupboard-bed 11. best room

g

d) A view of the interior of the Zeijen barn from the earth-packed threshing floor. Of particular interest is the framing of the structure by braced posts and beams, which will be seen again in the barns of New York State, except that the timbers here are rough-hewn from the tree trunks and lack the finish of timbers in the Dutch barns of the New World. The sapling-pole ceiling which forms the loft floor has its counterpart in the valley of the Hudson.

e) This wall was exposed in the restoration of the Zeijen barn, and shows well the ancient cob or wattle and daub construction.

f) The "living room" of the Zeijen barn is generous in space compared with Lichtenvoorde, and one can easily visualize the family gathered around the hearth. Their floor is cobbled up to the packed-earth threshing floor. A plain door leads to #11, which is described as the "best room", a step forward toward the goal of privacy.

g) The pigs in both barns flank the entrance, more, one would guess, to keep them distant than as posts of honour. In both plans, beds are shown in box-like compartments similar to modern folding beds, and are not a great improvement over the narrow wall beds in the Saxon house/barn. The hearth or fire-place was outside the partition and the temperature of the best room in winter can be imagined.

a

b

a) The "Larger Wemp" barn. (See pages 46–7.)

b) The great barn at New Lebanon in New York State, known as the "North Family Barn," is built of stone with slate roof, and is three hundred feet in length. Our view gives an indication of its scale by the presence of the carriage shed, itself no small building. The name is a reminder that it was built by the Shakers. At some point a change was made in the gable end, which was originally square-topped and subject to damage by water, a weakness in a building otherwise strong and weather-proof as a fortress.

c) The same barn seen from the lower level.

c

a

interest in a study of the Dutch barns of New York State. It will be noticed that timbers are roughly dressed, and frequently when bent they take the natural form of the tree from which they were cut, the rafters widely spaced and the poles resting on the anchor beams. Less conspicuous is the characteristic Dutch treatment of the beam ends, which project beyond the posts as a tongue often shaped to a semicircle. The wall construction finds no counterpart in the United States, but it is shown here because of its universal use, its antiquity as a technique, and its frequent use in Quebec during the seventeenth and early eighteenth centuries. It is the familiar wattle and daub, shown in the photograph, prior to the application of mud or plaster. All the features mentioned above, except the wall construction and the use of unsawn timber framing, were to find an echo in the Dutch barns beside the Hudson River.

Zeijen, like its fellow Lichtenvoorde, came from lush grass cattle country, and one has only to look at it to feel that centuries of experience and tradition, of weather in all its moods, of the needs of cattle and the simple comforts of the family, have gone into its design. It is a superb building the equal of any of the vernacular monuments of the world, and more than most, it is an organic thing, part and parcel of the earth.

Considerable space has been given in this book to those splendid barns that had been known to generations of the settlers who found their way to New York State and built their barns on lands bordering the Hudson, the Mohawk and the Schoharie rivers. In the pages that follow, it will be seen how much they owed in the design of their barns to the prototype at home. The miracle of the transfer of a culture from one continent to another is evident as much in the basic internal arrangements of threshing floor and aisles as in the magnificent timber framing of the New York Dutch barn.

The historic "New World" Dutch barns of the state have been most faithfully and painstakingly documented by Professor Fitchen, and interesting is his claim that all the barns listed in his survey are earlier than 1800; one at least may date from the seventeenth century, and that all the barns built subsequently are recognizable by different layout and different framing systems.[7]

In his opinion, all his "vintage" barns were built prior to the erection of a house, presumably of an adequate house, and the inadequacy of a log cabin temporary dwelling can be imagined. That there would be no diversion of effort from the stern requirements of the barn under construction can be gathered by an examination of its interior. The evidence is there of infinite patience, of precise craftsmanship by a few skilled hands.

Even a glance at the carefully fitted members in the framing of the Dutch barn will show that, however pressing the need for shelter, the work on the barn could not be accelerated any more than a cabinet maker could hasten the construction of a fine chest of drawers. With the help of a master carpenter, the farmer/builder would behold after weeks of work the great skeleton of his barn on the ground, and only then would the semi-skilled help of neighbours come into play. The erection of the frame, morticed and tenoned and pegged, entirely free from nails, even hand wrought, would be a day of triumph for all, but particularly the master carpenter.

Nowhere in this study of barn types can any be found as easy as the Dutch barn to analyze and lay before the reader. Points of similarity and difference between the prototype and the new are so very clear. Unlike other barn types, where the trail leading from a series of prototypes to the barn in the New World is often tortuous and hard to find, the end drive barn has left an unbroken trail from the Netherlands and Germany to New York State, and the features, qualities and functions of barns separated as they are by the Atlantic Ocean are not difficult to assess.

To attempt such an assessment, and to avoid a repetition of the words Prototype and New World, they are used only once as headings.

a) Unusual in North America is brick "nogging", or the filling of panels between the posts with brickwork. It is seen here in a stable in New York State. The floor boards were quite wide and four inches thick. Location: Schoharie, New York.

	PROTOTYPE	NEW WORLD

Dwelling:
The family lived in cramped but colourful quarters at the end of the barn: in earlier examples in an extension of the threshing floor, but later behind a wall with a communicating door to the livestock.

The Dutch immigrant from the beginning lived in a house removed from the barn.

The Entrance:
Characteristic was the entrance to the barns at one end, with, sometimes, a side entrance or exit to obviate the necessity for the wagon to back out. There was no possibility of an exit at the opposite end as that was effectively blocked by the "house part" or family quarters.

A door at each end of the barn was customary in the Dutch barns in New York State, and represented a major break with the old tradition of the single entrance. It enabled the wagon to pass through after unloading, and provided a draft for winnowing the grain from the ears of corn in the sheaf.

The Walls:
Walls consisted of timber posts with an infilling of brick, or that very ancient wall construction known as wattle and daub forming a bond for plaster.

Clapboard over studs. Boards were true boards and not tapered. Generally, clapboards were much wider than found in other barn types—11″ to 14″–and ⅞″ to 1½″ in thickness.[8]

Barn Dimensions:
Usually of composite shapes. (See plans.)

Nearly square in plan. A typical barn–the Somers barn in Upper Canada Village–measured 50′ x 45′

Eaves:
Low, often not the height of a man.

Examples measured varied from 13′6″ to 16′0″ which may be compared with barn types in other regions measuring 16′, 18′. Two barns followed the ancient custom of being low to the ground. They were the "larger Wemp" and the Schernmenham barns.

Roofs:
Roofs in the homeland are unforgettable, powerful, proof against all weathers, and marvellously manicured in reed thatch. They were hipped.

Cedar shingled and gabled.

Ground Floor:
Basically the basilican plan with nave and aisles. Universal were the central threshing floor with depressed aisles where the cattle stood facing the "nave" from which they were fed. The floor throughout was of hard packed earth.

With a plentiful supply of timber available, the threshing floor was built of thick planks and at no stage, so far as is known, was it packed earth. Like the prototype, the plan consisted of nave and aisles. No barn discovered or documented by Professor Fitchen is today performing its original function of housing livestock. That the aisles were used for cattle is proved by some being depressed from 1′6″ to 4′0″, precisely like those of the Old World. The animals stood on an earthen floor, faced into the threshing floor from which they were fed, and made their exit and their entrance at grade level through a door at the corner of the gable end of the barn.

Framing:
In the framing of the barn the transfer of an ancient building technique from one country to another is most evident. Illustrations show how complete the transfer was.

Framing of the Dutch barns in New York State is identical with those of Saxony and the Netherlands except that in the latter, some timbers (see illustration) take the form of the natural tree and were not sawn.

New York State should not be left without mention of the barn at New Lebanon, which would be an impressive piece of architecture in any country. It is built of stone (*c.* 1860) and is 300 feet long and five storeys in height. Access to the various floors was not possible, and research so far has failed to produce contemporary or later drawings. It is possible that this fortress-like building had some influence in plan and section on the very ingenious hillside barns of Vermont.

c

b) The interior of the barn above the stable, showing the aisle posts.

c) Another dramatic view of the North Family barn. Not visible is the central entrance door at the third-floor level, which is also the road level. There are five storeys in all.
Location: same as 43*b*.

a

b

c

d

a,b c) Nowhere in these pages is the contrast so great between the modest, unimpressive exterior and the spectacular, spacious interior as in the so-called "Larger Wemp" barn. Of particular interest to those struck by this masterpiece of barn-framing are the long continuous rafters (not jointed at the purlin), the absence of a ridge board, and the tongue of the anchor beam morticed and pegged with oak as it passes through the post. The anchor beam is given even further security by oak pegs driven hard against the post, and, in an unusual refinement, the diagonal braces are chamfered.

d) With its different members in tension and compression, there is still a serenity in the framework of the Dutch barn. Interesting is the contrast between the precise carpentry of beams, posts and braces and the old land tradition of sapling poles for the loft floor—never, unless by accident, touching. Space between them provided ventilation for the hay.

a

b

48

c

d

a) The Schermerhorn barn in New York State is no longer extant, and many elements in its make-up have no relation to the barn in the Netherlands. Still, it is valuable as a record of how basically many barns in the state, now lost, must have appeared. Its eaves are low, the roof is steep, the wagon doors are in the right place, and the side doors show where the cattle and horses made their exit from sunken floors flanking the nave from which they were fed. The clapboard, louvred windows, and projecting barge boards on the gable are not original.

b) One of the most successful park museums anywhere is Upper Canada Village, which comprises buildings of many types that would otherwise have perished in the widening of the St. Lawrence River Ship Canal. This "Schoharie" barn is one of only two that we know of in Canada that are still in worthwhile condition and now in the Village. Both are longer than the New World Dutch barn and higher in the eaves than the prototype in the Netherlands, but they have the characteristic central door and framing. The pitch of the roof has been anglicized in Ontario.

c) This New York State barn shows the characteristic true Dutch features missing in the Schoharie barn in Ontario. It will be noticed that the eaves are low, the side door in the gable wall is the cows' exit, and the pitch of the roof is close to that of the better known Schermerhorn barn.

d) Staphorst is another of the delightful barns now restored in the open air museum at Arnhem. Here we see the sunken pit where the cattle stood and the threshing floor into which they looked for feeding.

49

a

b

c

a) The ramp on the right indicates the approach to the mow, the floor of which would be the ceiling of byre and stable. The roof is gambrel slightly hipped at the peak, with three "spikey" little ventilators on the ridge. The walls are plank.
Location: near St.-Jean-de-Dieu, Quebec.

b) A late form of the Dutch barn near Cicero, New York.

c) Very rare indeed in North America is the compact house where the family lived under the same roof as animals and fodder. In this interesting example, still extant, the living quarters were twenty feet in depth and consisted of two storeys, the upper being bedrooms. All the ground floor rooms had windows overlooking the barn. Dated 1906.
Location: fourteen miles northwest of Weyburn, Saskatchewan.

d) The exterior of this barn gives no clue to its remarkably efficient interior. It is placed right on the

edge of the country road, and its ramp reaches the threshing floor under cover. One feature of this barn, for which the owner expressed to us his indebtedness to his grandfather who built it, is that the hay from the wagon is pitched down with speed and ease and not up. Naturally, there were others in Vermont who adopted so excellent a technique.
Location: near Waitsfield, Vermont.

e) The octagonal cupola on the same barn sits squarely on the ridge, surrounded by a superb textured

d

e

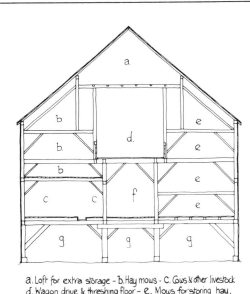

a. Loft for extra storage - b. Hay mows - c. Cows & other livestock
d. Wagon drive & threshing floor - e. Mows for storing hay,
grain & other storage - f. feeding passage - g. Manure basement.

f

roof of cedar shingles.

f) The section tells the interesting story of gravity feed
to the cattle and horses from the threshing floor above.
Location: same as *d*.

g) The section should be examined along with this
view of the interior of the barn. It will be seen that
nothing but a parapet separates the threshing floor
from the sunken mow into which the hay is dropped.
Location: same as *d*.

g

a

b

c

d

a) Basically this is an ordinary barn of the Victorian era, but its charm derives from a number of features such as the gabled dormers and the unexpected (and perhaps not too useful) sash windows. The roof may be described as a hipped gable, and the walls are board and batten. The central door marked the carriage entrance.
Location: Madoc, Ontario.

b, c) The gambrel-roofed barn appears late in the nineteenth century or early in the present one. In this barn, too, the principle of gravity feed to the byre two or three floors below has been used, and one's surprise is great when the streetfront entrance to the drive floor is compared with the four-storey façade at the bottom of the hill. In all, there are three levels of entrance to this barn.
Location: Route A, near Bridgewater, Vermont.

d) Everything is present in this barn to satisfy the most discriminating taste—its setting in the immediate landscape and the hills beyond, the colour and texture of the vertical boards, and the way in which they contrast with the lighter shingled roof and the matching little silo. Vernacular architecture of the highest order.
Location: south of Rochester, Vermont.

a

a) This barn might well have found a place in the Museum of Modern Art exhibit entitled "Architecture without Architects." It is a handsome structure, from the shadowed cattle floor to the frieze below the eave. We can also enjoy the simplicity of the main wall, relieved as it is by the slightly projecting shuttered doors, which provide ventilation for the hay mow.

b) Interior of a.

c) Interior of a, seen from the longitudinal drive floor, showing the high hay mows.

d) Plan of barn floor.

e) Rather like a theatre set is the granary in which three arches face another three in just the right atmosphere for drama. It will be realized that boards pile one on another as the bins are filled. This barn is in a

b

c

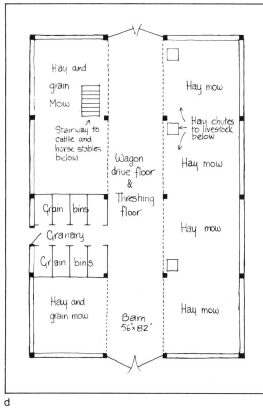

Hay and grain Mow

Stairway to cattle and horse stables below

Grain bins

Granary

Grain bins

Hay and grain mow

Wagon drive floor & Threshing floor

Barn 56'x82'

Hay mow

Hay chutes to livestock below

Hay mow

Hay mow

Hay mow

d

class of small fine vernacular buildings that might in any country be declared a national monument. Unfortunately it is too frail a thing to outlast this century or even decade.

e

"Change and decay in all around I see..."

a

a) The English barn on North American soil, proof
against wind and weather. Ventilation is provided by
embrasures in the gable end and the two louvred
"windows" on the front. The barn measures 60' x
33'6'' and is 18'0'' high to the eave.
Location: Fourth Line, Nassagaweya, Ontario.

The English Barn

Chapter 2

Small English Barn.

b

b) A drawing taken from a British Report on Agriculture published in 1798, and designed to be built in brick. Bricks were omitted for ventilation and took the diamond pattern seen on each side of the door to the threshing floor. In the chapter on the Pennsylvania barn, it will be seen to what extent this simple device was exploited.

This little barn, also known as the three-bay or the Yankee, is as ubiquitous as the English sparrow. It is a type widely known in Europe, and was brought to the New World by farmers of different nationalities – more particularly by the English, who introduced it to New England whence it spread to the Midwest and to Canada.

Nothing could be simpler or more modest in appearance and plan, and at first sight the reader may wonder why it can be classed in interest or in age with, say, the spectacular barns of Pennsylvania. In terms of age, it is known to have existed in England in the seventeenth century, if not earlier. By the year 1797, it was so well established that it was described and illustrated as a model in a British report on agriculture, and given the title of an English barn.[1]

In the handsome drawing included in the report, the barn consisted of two mows and a threshing floor. "ab" is a cross wall about 3'0" high, built to separate the threshed from the unthreshed corn, and "e" of the same height is for the storage of sheaves waiting their turn. It is open to the threshing floor, but covered with boards. The barn is designed for brick, and very interesting is the pattern formed by the omission of bricks. This was a device to provide ventilation, and in the great barns of Pennsylvania it can be seen to what lengths this technique was successfully exploited.

In so simple and forthright a structure, the evolutionary processes that gave it form since the seventeenth century can have been few. Its publication by a government agricultural board in 1797 would suggest a knowledge of its usefulness in the past and its promise for the century immediately ahead.

From the scale on the drawing, the barn would appear to measure 55' x 25', in width not unlike a modest suburban lawn. These dimensions are of interest because a ratio of 2:1 or 60' x 30' is not uncommon in the small North American barn.

From a study of the plan it will be gathered that the three-bay barn did not lend itself to an operation that combined the housing of livestock as well as threshing and crop storage. It flourished during the period when wheat cultivation dominated the agricultural economy.

In many parts of the United States, especially in the region of the Southern Moun-

a

a) A little barn that has sheltered many a harvest, but now in retirement. It has aged with time, but the logs and the shingles were there at its birth. Many early Ontario barns took this form.

b) The threshing floor bent gives support to both structure and hay.

b

a

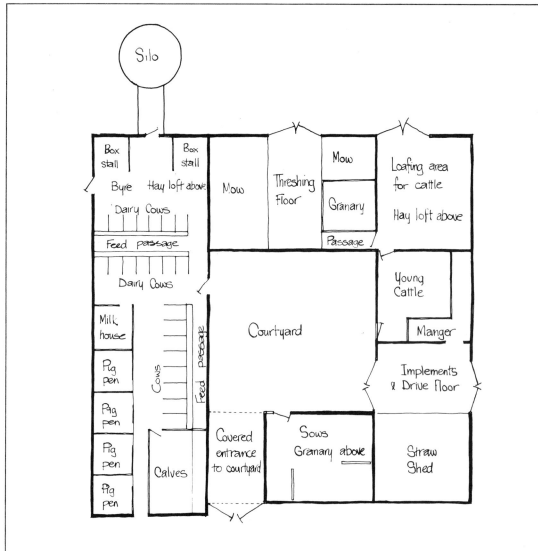

b

tains, the three-bay barn in its basic form contained livestock on one side and storage on the other, and this would be true of very small farms in Canada and the United States.

Writing of the Yankee barn in Ontario, Peter Ennals notes that "it was admirably suited to the level of technology and the scale of operation which characterized wheat agriculture in Ontario." That could doubtless be said of the same barn in the United States and Great Britain under similar economic circumstances. He says further: "on the kind of farm where the operation was such as to justify nothing more commodious than the two-bay barn,[2] the procedure for harvesting was to store the cut but unthreshed grain in the barn until the farmer had time to deal with it. The amount of grain produced on an early farm probably rarely filled the average barn. Little additional space was required, and, if it proved insufficient, the farmer could always build a rick."[3]

After 1850, a change in the agricultural economy from wheat to livestock affected the three-bay barn in several ways. A stable or byre could be added giving the barn greater length, or the necessary addition could be placed to form an ell. The happiest solution, and one that gives distinction to many a farmstead, is the disposal of buildings about a court.

The British agricultural reform movement of the late eighteenth century recommended the linking of buildings to effect obvious economies in travel. In North America this usually took the form of the linear or connected barn, but in the literature of the subject in Britain, most writers urged the claims of the courtyard. Many of the illustrated proposals included the house, and not a few were fanciful, even ludicrous in conception rather than practical.

The completely enclosed barn yard in North America must be considered rare, but the three-sided is common. The sketch in this chapter of an actual farmstead in Ontario requires no explanation, as the pattern and the function of each of the ancillary buildings will be apparent. What needs to be described in detail is the barn itself at the head of the group. The mow on the left and the threshing floor will be recognized, but what is not revealed in the plan is that the threshing floor continues unobstructed through to the

a, b) Unlike the L and ∩ plans, the □ or enclosed court is rare. This one is built of log in an area where some of the finest log barns are to be found.
Location: near Carleton Place, Ontario.

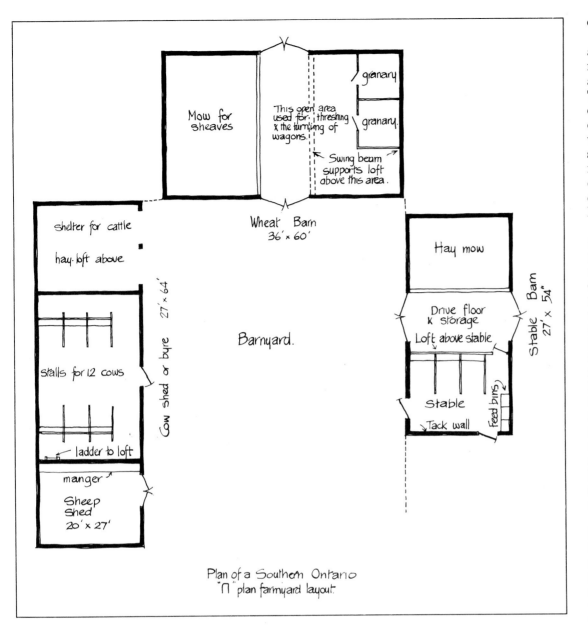

granary

granary

Mow for
sheaves

This open area
used for threshing
& the turning of
wagons.

← Swing beam
supports loft
above this area.

Wheat Barn
36' x 60'

shelter for cattle

hay-loft above

stalls for 12 cows

← ladder to loft

manger

Sheep
Shed
20' x 27'

Cow shed or byre 27' x 64'

Barnyard.

Hay mow

Drive floor
& storage

Loft above stable

Stable

Tack wall

Feed bins

Stable Barn 27' x 54"

Plan of a Southern Ontario
"Π" plan farmyard layout.

outer wall and bins.

This enlargement of the threshing floor by a bay is a striking change from the British model of 1797, where bays and threshing floor are, except for doors, separate compartments. The North American farmer made use of the enlarged free space for threshing and storage of implements, but it was not achieved without a structural innovation of great significance. Over the extended floor is a loft for the storage of fodder, and its support comes principally and visibly from a major element in the framing of the barn, a timber known as the swing beam.

One cannot but feel in the interior of many of the barns in these pages that one is in the presence of great architecture, but no one would expect any surprise, let alone an uplift of the spirit, inside a three-bay barn. The surprise is there in the diagonal view one gets when standing at the left hand corner of the open doors and looking at the beam and the loft. All our barn types have their grand timbers, whether posts or beams, and all recall a time when trees from the neighbouring forest provided straight timbers up to sixty feet in length and of impressive sections; but none is quite as striking as the uninterrupted swing beam. This powerful member in the framing of the barn takes nearly the full load of floor and fodder, besides serving as the principal member of a sturdy truss to support the loft and help contain the hay or sheaves.

In the transfer of the Yankee barn from Britain to New England with its different needs, climate and materials, the swing beam and the loft are perhaps the most significant, though not the most conspicuous changes from the prototype. By the end of the eighteenth century in England, few barns would be built of wood, and the majority would be of brick or stone. Mr. Anthony Garvan is of the opinion that the technique of frame construction, as we know it, in the barns and domestic architecture of North America can be traced to the earliest settlers in New England. Essex was the birth place of many of these immigrants, and was a county in England with a long tradition of building in wood.[4]

In *The Log Cabin Myth*, Mr. Shurtleff disposes of the commonly held view that the earliest buildings in the new world were of log. They were of clapboard. His references

a

a) A charming group of senior citizens. The contour of
the ground, log walls and moss-covered shingles leave
an unforgettable impression.
Location: near Killaloe, Ontario.

b

b) A picturesque scene caused by additions to the old
original; the barn is on the right.
Location: near Dacre, Ontario.

c) The English barn and the wheat waiting to be
garnered.

c

a

b

c

from contemporary documents are numerous, including one in which Governor Winthrop in 1632 writes, "Mr. Oldham had a small house near the weir at Watertown, made all of clapboards, burnt down by making a fire in it when it had no chimney."[5] And from Canada, there is a revealing account in "Master John Guy his letter to Master Slany Treasurer, and to the Counsel of the New-found-land Plantation," dated 1611, in which he writes of building activity at the Bay of Conception: "a second sawpit at the fresh lake standing within twelve score of our Habitation to saw the timber...in keeping two paire of Sawyers to saw plankes for the said buildings...in making the frame of timber of a fairer house than that which as yet we live in."[6] The reference to sawpits, sawyers and "plankes," and so early a use of the word 'frame', leads inevitably to a picture of the "fairer" house sheathed in boards.

Whether the planks were laid horizontally as clapboard, or vertically like board and batten, is not known. The walls were not log.

Mr. Shurtleff, Mr. Fiske Kimball and other architectural historians have shown conclusively that "the English colonies throughout the seventeenth century, were complete strangers to the log cabin, a form of construction that was brought to America by the Swedes who settled on the Delaware in 1638...and, independently by the Germans in 1710."[7] Log cabins or barns of the eighteenth century may exist in the United States and Canada, but virtually all known barns are nineteenth-century.

The English tradition of building in wood took two forms in North America – the well tried clapboard on studs, and plank in vertical boards. The latter may have been the sheathing for the "fairer" house in Newfoundland, and, while the three-bay barn is found in stone in Pennsylvania, it is less common than vertical siding.[8] Rather surprisingly, considering the popularity of clapboard in narrow boards and log in a wide variety of early barn types, they take second place to vertical boards in eastern North America including Ontario.

A curious survival from the age of thatch is the steep roof of the New England barn, with a pitch of 45 degrees or more. The use of cedar shingles or slate would suggest a roof of gentler slope as it did in England when tile and slate superseded thatch, but the steep roof in New England persisted through the nineteenth century. Considerable numbers of Empire Loyalists came to Upper Canada from the south following the American Revolution, and considering their close ties with Britain, it should not be unexpected that the roof of the barn in that early period followed the English pattern of gentle pitch, or "one third" in the language of the carpenter.

The bay in its architectural sense goes back more than two millennia. When the Celts in Britain in the fourth century B.C. used their crucks in the building of a house or barn, they spaced them in bays. It is a term quite unrelated to bay windows or oriels, and may describe the spacing of arches in the cathedrals of the Middle Ages or the intervals between steel columns in a modern office building.

It is a term in universal use by architects and engineers. In early times, two things

a) The swing beam was an entirely North American element in the English barn, and came about because of the extension of the threshing floor by a bay with a loft overhead for the storage of fodder. The appearance of many an English barn gives no indication that within is a swing beam of awesome dimensions, dating from a time when nearby pine forests produced trees of gigantic size. For an unusually bountiful harvest, an additional floor was put over the threshing floor. The square holes show where the joists were fitted for its support.

Location: Highway 25, near Milton, Ontario.

b) The same swing beam in detail showing the beauty of the surface of the timber as it was finished by the carpenter's adze. The beam is 34'0" long and 2'4½" deep.
Location: same as a.

c) A beautifully fitted beam, morticed and tenoned into the post with oak pegs. The detail shows with what precision the beam is "boxed" or let into the post, and

the scribing lines of the carpenter are still faintly visible.
Location: same as a.

a

b

c

d

e

a) The wagon doors open to the threshing floor. In the foreground is the weathered framework that once held the straw rick.

b) This is a nineteenth-century scene with the architectural atmosphere of an even earlier time. Though appearing L-shaped, it is actually a ∩ with protection for the cattle when they are outside in winter. A silo peeps over the valley formed by the two roofs.
Location: near Carleton Place, Ontario.

c) This is an ingenious example of sway and compression bracing as resistance to wind pressure. The three braces are seen forming a triangle between a vertical member of a bent and the swing beam.
Location: same as d.

d) An intersection in the framing where the tie beam is morticed into the corner post, and the post into the plate.
Location: Sixth Concession, Vaughan Township, Ontario.

e) Close-up of d.

contributed to the bay width in the barn–one was determined by the weight of the roof which originally would be reed thatch, and the other was the desirable width for a standing cow or ox. From time immemorial the width of a stall has been four feet, or seven feet for a yoke of oxen in a double stall. Writing in Rome in 11 B.C., Vitruvius said: "The standing room for each pair of oxen should be not less than seven feet," and Palladius, on the same subject in 210 A.D., found "eight feet more than sufficient for each yoke of oxen."

It was from such an inherited background as this that the English barn took its form, and even the bay which remains a fairly constant width in North America may have been governed by housing two oxen or two cows.

The three-bay barn in its form, use, and construction may be summarized as follows:

Name:
It is known in different parts of the United States and Canada as the three-bay barn, English barn, or Connecticut barn.

Form:
It takes its form from the English barn of the late eighteenth century–a simple basic shape approximately sixty feet in length with a central pair of doors back and front, a gable at each end, and an uninterrupted roof ridge.

Plan A:
Where farm operation required nothing more of the barn than a threshing floor, and space for the storage of sheaves or hay and implements, the plan consisted of a bay to the left for storage of sheaves before threshing, a threshing floor extended to the right to accommodate implements, and a loft.

Plan B:
Under different circumstances such as an enlargement of the farmer's operation to include cattle and horses, the barn might be extended to right or left, or, alternatively, a wing on one side forming an ell would give protection to the yard from the prevailing wind. With still further development, the possibility was present for an impressive architectural layout such as a ∩ or □.

Materials:
Of almost universal use are vertical siding

and shingled roofs. A characteristic feature of the frame three-bay barn is the fact that boarding, whether horizontal or vertical, comes close to the ground. A sill is set on a very low wall or on stone piers, and the bottom nailing of the boards is in the sill. The wall is just high enough to prevent rot.

It is not uncommon for barns in New England to be painted, and sometimes embellished by cupolas and pigeon roosts, but for the rest of eastern North America, the three-bay barn of grey weathered boards, stark against the sky line, is a more familiar sight.

The Double Crib Barn. The double crib barn fits perfectly into a chapter on the three-bay barn. In fact, in elevation where both are of log construction, it is impossible to distinguish between the two. There are, however, points of difference going deeper than mere façade. Mention has been made of the wide range of the English barn and its limited use for the storage of fodder and for threshing. By contrast, the territory in which the double crib barn is found is limited. A recent article[9] describes, generally, the area where the majority are found, or, more specifically, throughout the Southern Mountains. Other points of difference are these:

THE DOUBLE CRIB BARN: CONSTRUCTION	THE THREE-BAY OR ENGLISH BARN:
In the older examples construction was invariably of log. Corners were treated in several ways, but the horizontal logs forming the wall were not tight jointed: i.e. they were not chinked, and installation was achieved without louvres or other aids.	The majority are vertical plank, but examples are found in clapboard, log, and cedar shingle.
Doors	
As the space between the cribs was a runway with access to the cribs on each side, doors were unnecessary. Where they are found, the runway was a driveway and, probably, served as a threshing floor, which at times would be closed at both ends.	Doors to front and rear are universal on the three-bay barn.
Use	
It was common practice to reserve one crib for cows and one for stabling.	There was no provision for cattle or other livestock in the basic English barn.

f

f) Detail of a wedged mortice-and-tenon joint.

a

a) This delightful barn is in Blount County, Tennessee. It consists of two cribs supporting a loft which is cantilevered front, back, and sides. The structural principle on which it is based is as modern as anything in the field of building technology.

Always there was a loft for the storage of hay.

Plan

In spite of the simplicity of the barn façade formed by the two equal masses framing the runway opening, there is quite a variation in plan arrangement.

1. Two rectangular cribs face each other so that the doors open on the runway.

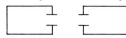

2. In type 2 there is a variety of plan shapes from the simple oblong to the square. Doors may open on the driveway or as shown in the sketch, on the front.

3. Type 3 may be looked on as two large cribs each

There are no significant variations in the plan of the three-bay barn. It should also be noted that its plan was not as simple as it might first appear. It will be remembered that there was no partition in the right-hand bay for convenience in threshing, and that over it, and it alone, was a loft.

divided in the middle with four doors opening on the driveway.

N.B. Each of these types, like the three-bay barns, have gable ends.

In his scholarly study of the barn in Appalachia, Dr. Glassie is of the opinion that type 3 is most common and type 1 least. As it was general practice to reserve one crib for cows and the other for stabling, the greater flexibility in type 3 with its four compartments is apparent. In each case there was a loft for the storage of hay reached from doors opening on the driveway.

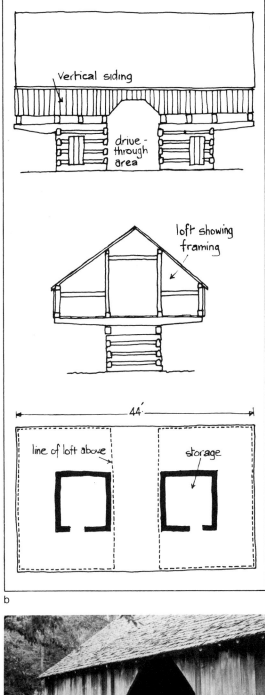

Vertical siding

drive-
through
area

loft showing
framing

44'

line of loft above

storage

b

d

c

b) Front and side elevations and plan in diagram form.

c) Detail of the cantilever showing in shadow the door entrance to the crib.

d) Another crib barn, with overhang supported on posts.
Location: Cade's Cove, Tennessee.

a

b

c

a) The origin of this barn would seem to be in Pennsylvania rather than New England, but, because it is a single-storey double crib, it is included in this chapter. The decision of the builder to cantilever was a curious one, as little was gained in accommodation, and the cost of construction over traditional methods was considerable. Looked at from a purely aesthetic viewpoint, it is a very interesting barn.
Location: Black Creek Pioneer Village, Toronto.

b) An interior of the same barn showing one log crib.

c) The cantilever is formed by massive beams at close centres. They rest on sleepers which, in turn, rest on squat stone piers.

d

e

f

d) The basic English barn form—low pitched roof and clapboard, the boards being warped with age and stiffened with battens.

e) A not unfamiliar sight: the old frame barn has been jacked up to sit over a stone byre. The wagon entrance, now boarded up, has become only a memory of bygone harvests.
Location: Ballinafad, Ontario.

f) Boulders giving added strength and interest to the dry wall of flat river-type stone masonry.

a

a) To be noted here is the almost universal design of
the doors with ''standard'' post, the mow poles resting
on the tie beams, and the deep plank partition below
the swing beam.
Location: Milliken, Ontario.

b

c

d

b) The same barn, showing hand-hewn rafters supporting the broad planks on the roof. Generally, rafters were sawn or were saplings trimmed of branches. Sometimes they were tapered and achieved an elegance that was pleasant to see but contributed nothing to the stability of the structure. It is not unlikely that the taper came in the first place from the diminishing thickness of the tree from which the rafter was cut.

c) A hand-forged hook and eye, from the same barn. The hook is bent to meet the eye in the post, giving extra strength to the hook.

d) The wagon doors, of interest chiefly for the hook and eye which fasten them, and the "standard" to which the doors are attached. This post has an almost universal use, and is fitted to a hole in the beam above and in the ground below. Being loose, it could be removed when both doors were required open.

a

a) There are few more tragic sights to be seen in the countryside than a great barn complex permitted to fall into decay. These buildings, fine in themselves, were arranged, as we shall see, about a court. They were of stone, in a district famous for its stone and its Scottish masons.
Location: outside the village of Arkell, Ontario.

b

c

d

b) Even without the protection of a roof, the mason's arch remained intact.
Location: same as *a*.

c) The impressive court consisted of stables on the left, the barn centre, and the cow byre on the right. There are still elderly neighbours who remember this great group of buildings in its prime.
Location: same as *a*.

d) Inside the ruins: rusting machinery and unravelling ropes dangling from a windlass.
Location: same as *a*.

a) A picturesque ∩-shaped court that can still give an idea of its former glory. On the left is a rather romantic stair that led to a granary with a dormer giving protection to the door and landing. Below was a sheep barn and stable, and across the end, the cow byre. The barn occupied all of the right hand side.
Location: Black's Corners, Ontario.

b) An impressive picture of weather-beaten logs so locked together that one gets the impression of the strength in masonry of the quoin.

c

d

e

c) JOHN W
RISEBROU
        GH
carves his name on a beam.
The old cemeteries show many examples of the care-
lessness of sculptor/masons in allowing for letters in a
line. The farmer often failed to solve the same problem,
but how charming for us to see his error a hundred
years later.
Location: Sixth Line, Markham Township, Ontario.

d) Not at all apparent here is a master carpenter's
device where a narrow channel is cut into the bottom
of the beam to hold the heads of the planks firmly in
position without nailing.

e) The triple bracing on the cross beam and the
scissor bracing between the posts are an example of
skilful work in the carpentry and erection of this barn.
Location: Milliken, Ontario.

a

b

a) Much pleasure can be got out of an analysis of this barn. Both the open-gable hay doors and the snug little silo top are perfect in their setting. Rather forlorn, but charming, is the pair of doors to the stable, which are designed in a chevron pattern. In addition, of course, is the colour of the barn and the fragrance of cedar logs mingling with the more earthy odours of the yard.

b) Before the day of the mail-order hardware catalogue, a latch in wood was often carved by hand for the standard post that separated the wagon doors.

c

c) Another view of the log barn, which shows the silo on the end silhouetted against the sky like a lookout on a medieval castle.

d) This is an example of the extensive use of hand-made wooden pegs, used here (a) to hold the rafter end from moving on the plate and (b) to hold the plate firmly to the upper log.

d

a

a) *Le grange anglais du Québec.*
Location: Charlevoix County.

b) The farmer's boat, resting keel-high in grass on a
threshing floor that once resounded to the beat of
flailers' blows.
Location: near Carluke, Ontario.

c) The threshing floor exposed.

b

c

d

d) At first sight, a very ordinary gable end to an English barn. Unusual, and a sign of age, is the laying of the narrow clapboard in short lengths arranged like bricks so that vertical joints from one board to the one below or above are avoided. Two pigeon holes provide access for the pigeons and a mite of ventilation.

e) A rather spectacular view from the hay mow, with the familiar swing beam in place. The purlins which support the rafters and run parallel to the sides of the barn get bracing from struts morticed into the tie beam.

e

A late sophisticated expression of the Pennsylvania
barn in Ontario. It was designed by an architect whose
drawings and handwritten specifications are extant. He
demonstrates his skill particularly in the elegance of
the cupola. The elliptical arched opening was the
entrance to the manure shed.
Location: north of Crewson's Corners, Ontario. (See
also page 227.)

The Pennsylvania Barn

Chapter 3

The story of the barn in North America is brief if thought of in terms of its development since the days of settlement in the United States and Canada, but ancient enough against the background of its origins in Europe. In this chapter, we are looking particularly at Pennsylvania (with a sidelong glimpse of Ontario), which in the seventeenth, eighteenth and nineteenth centuries became home for people of such different racial origins as English, French, Irish, Scots, Welsh, and Dutch, as well as Germans from the Rhineland and Swiss from many an alpine village.

At first sight, the variety of these ethnic groups and their regional divisions and subdivisions, not to mention the diversity of their cultures, present a formidable barrier to the recognition of those national architectural characteristics that one would hope to uncover in the barns on the soil of North America.

The chapter on the Dutch barn demonstrated the indisputable influence on the immigrant Dutch of the barns of their homeland. But the influences at work in Pennsylvania and Ontario are vastly more complex, and not, for the layman, immediately discernible. Important in any study of the barn in North America is the three-bay or English barn which is to be found on both sides of the border, and in various states and provinces of Canada, but when one thinks of the two-level barn, the *ne plus ultra* of banked barns, the one that immediately comes to mind is the Pennsylvania barn.

While more than once in these pages reference has been made to the paucity of information, historic, economic, and aesthetic on the barn, it has been noted earlier that no such charge can be made against Pennsyl-
vania. The literature of the state is rich in the publication of folklore magazines; folklore societies thrive and great universities have faculties staffed by art historians, geographers, and architects, whose principal concern is the cultural history of the state and the dissemination of knowledge on a wide variety of subjects. In this, the barn as an artifact plays a distinctly important role, which may be traced in spite of the diverse cultures of successive waves of immigrants over the last three hundred years. Fortunately, the task was made less difficult by the fact that the dominant groups were Swiss and German, and historians have come to agree that the banked barn of the state comes from a marriage of their two cultures.

Thomas Wertenbaker, a very acute observer, writes: "we must seek the ancestry of the Pennsylvania-German barn in the wooded highlands of Upper Bavaria, the southern spurs of the Black Forest mountains, in the Jura region and elsewhere in Switzerland."[1] All have something in common, and all bring us back to the barn in Pennsylvania except for one fundamental deviation from the prototype. Each owed its form to the terrain, but where those mountain European barns were built at right angles to the lie of the hill, the New World barn was, from the beginning, set parallel to it.

Points of similarity were structural rather than domestic, and, to take the Upper Bavarian house/barns first, living arrangements are found to be similar to those ancient Netherlands barns where the family quarters on the ground floor were in close proximity to the livestock. The Bavarian farmer shared the barn with his animals all under one roof, but with the difference that his house of two storeys, with charming windows, quaint-carved designs in wood, and a balcony, was a separate entity. Placed at the barn head overlooking a valley, it had all the appearance of the prow of a ship. Its importance architecturally was emphasized by the gable end of the great roof which was held down by boulders against the force of the mountain winds. Behind the house, digging into the hill and stretching back for eighty or a hundred feet, was the combined barn and byre. The lower floor is assigned to horses, cattle and oxen, the stalls being laid out along aisles entered from doors in the long side of the structure. The lower floor is

a

a) The Dalziel barn is one of the finest log barns left in North America. It is now a museum piece, unspoilt except for the windows visible in the mow. It bears a stone with the date 1809. Note the overhanging mow, called a *laube* or "overshoot," which protects the byre wall and shelters the animals underneath in inclement weather.
Location: Black Creek Pioneer Village on the outskirts of Toronto.

b) The Baker barn, with a stone dated 1822. The view is of the log loft above the threshing floor now holding farm implements of a bygone age.
Location: Concord, Ontario. (See page 94.)

b

a

usually of stone, and the super-structure housing the hayloft and threshing floor of hewn logs.

So characteristic were the features of the Bavarian house that Wertenbaker could say, "we could follow this house far through the Alps from Upper Bavaria to the valley of the Inn, thence through Vorarlberg to Bern."[2] With the Swiss house there were many areas of resemblance. There was a common tradition of building in heavy timbers, and a love of colour which, with carving, was used with effect on the front of the house, and, like the others, was in the forefront with the barn behind. Livestock were kept in their stalls at grade level, and the mow and threshing floor above were entered from the hill or by a ramp. There are many variations of the Swiss house both in floor arrangement and construction. Older houses were all of log, but they, in turn, gave place to the stone stable and log mow. Not unknown are homesteads where the house is completely separated from the barn.

Many of the Swiss were Mennonites, and in their enforced departure from persecution at home many have left their Swiss High-

lands, crossed the Upper Rhine and made their way into the Black Forest. There a different house evolved, but still one closely akin to the Swiss. It had a "huge hipped roof falling on either side often forty or fifty feet, unbroken by dormers, and giving it the appearance of a Noah's ark grounded on the side of a hill."[3] It departed from both the Swiss and the Bavarian houses in its interior arrangements. Animals were still in their familiar position at ground level, but above it were two floors designed for the exclusive use of the family. Over all was the mow, an unbroken space from end to end of the building, and approached like the Swiss and the Bavarian barns at an upper level. Wertenbaker looked in vain for a chimney from the kitchen hearth below the hay. There was none, and the "smoke rose into the loft under the roof where it is said to protect the beams from destruction by worms, to cure the corn and fodder, and, finally to filter through the thatch, or out through a ventilator."[4]

With such a background, it would not be assuming too much to speculate that we can recognize in the design of the Pennsylvania barn an amalgam of many of the features that were characteristic of barns in the homeland cherished for generations by the immigrants to North America. Especially would this be true where a family line could be traced to Switzerland or Bavaria. For the Mennonites, for example, carpentry was a specialized trade and the skills that were required of them in Europe would be demanded again in Pennsylvania.

There is something fascinating about the transfer of cultural traditions from the old world to the new. So marked are they that Wertenbaker could say "there is no possibility of confusing the Dutch barn with the German or the English barn. As one motors westward from New Brunswick and sees an old barn with the wagon entrance on the long side, he may be certain it is of English or New England antecedents; if the entrance is in the gable it is Dutch, and, when after crossing the Delaware, he finds barns with the stables on the ground floor and the threshing floor above, he knows it is a Pennsylvania Swiss or German barn."[5]

In spite of the age-long tradition of the dwelling in juxtaposition to the livestock in the barn, the custom was shortlived in the United States. Some question that it ever

b

a,b) Another view of the Dalziel barn. (See 86a.) The barn measures 50' x 28', and the mow overhang is 8'0''. The windows are a recent addition.

c) A Bavarian peasant's house showing the balcony at the head of the barn. Boulders hold the roof down against mountain winds. Not as pronounced as the *laube* in the Pennsylvania barn is the second floor projection which, though for a different purpose, doubtless influenced the immigrant in the New World.

existed. However, it is known that in 1643 Jacob van Curler wrote Killiaen van Rensslaer saying he had contracted with the carpenter Jan Cornelissen for a farmhouse 120 feet long by twenty-eight feet wide; "forty of the length being used for the dwelling and the rest to house the labourers, cattle, and horses. The whole was to be thatched with reed."[6]

The reasons for the abandonment of the house/barn combination must have been several, the chief one being the heat from the animals in an American summer. Always, too, there was the danger from fire – especially if, with timber there for the taking in the forest, burning logs were to replace the smouldering peat on the hearths of the homeland fire.

Of particular interest to us in a study of the Pennsylvania barn is the laube or forebay, an overshoot of the barn floor affording an enclosed gallery above and a protection to the walls, windows and doors below. This very typical feature of the barn in Pennsylvania is found in only a limited projection in the Upper Bavarian barn, and is not to be confused with the cantilevered mow

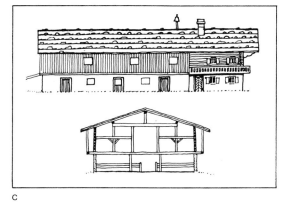

c

of eight or ten feet in the New World. It is true that in North America there are barns where the mow projection is so restricted as to do little more than give protection to the wall below, and the same rather ineffective overhang, often terminated by corbels at the gable ends, can be seen in old cottages in Salem. Whether the extension of the upper floor space was to gain a few added square feet to protect the structure beneath, or whether it can be attributed to nostalgic memories of home in Europe, is not known, but one writer speaks of its European origins as follows:

"It is of interest that military architecture had always made use of the extended, overhanging framed bay. The tourist may still visit the walled towns of Britain, France and Germany and see this form of construction in place. The towns of northern Europe were characterized by such defense works and even the irregular narrow streets and ways were lined with tall houses which extended forward above the traffic. From the countryside of Southern Germany, the Rhine Pfalz and Switzerland came a majority of the farming settlers, folk used to deep valleys, wide ranging hills and mountains where the 'bank' structure was an accepted solution for a variety of buildings. Not only were there banked hay barns but houses and even churches and public buildings were entered from grade at various levels. Thus the gathered hills, mantled everywhere in endless superb forests, suggested to the earliest German refugees and settlers a solution combined of time-tested elements and present demands, projecting a new form—the great 'bank' barn of Pennsylvania."[7]

The characteristic forebay of the Pennsylvania barn was a bolder piece of construction, and its use is patently clear when the cattle are seen sunning themselves in lazy comfort on a windy day in winter. In its typical form the banked barn was built into a hill with its long axis parallel to the hilltop, and, considering the practical possibilities of the forebay as a shelter for cattle in appropriate weather, it was desirable that the barn faced south.

The upper storey is by ancient custom generally described as the threshing floor, but the area where that operation once took place, and sheaves were beaten with the flail, is now called the drive floor. In a mechanized

d) The byre wall in the Francey barn near Toronto showing the cantilevered logs and the closed end to the sheltered space. Wall logs and beams are of immense size, cut in the 1840's from a convenient pine forest.
Location: near Victoria Square, Markham Township, Ontario.

d

a

b

c

a) The stone ends of the barn are flush with the fore-bay. This is a type of barn found particularly in the southeastern parts of the state. A façade of great simplicity. The doors indicate the end of the threshing floor. They are smaller than the wagon doors on the hilltop side, and when opened in a favourable breeze provided the draft necessary for separating the grain from the chaff.
Location: same as *a*.

b) A great Pennsylvania barn on its own soil. In comparison to the massive stone wall, the doors to the stable seem almost light-hearted, with their almost Chinese protective hoods and the gothicized palladian window in the gable.
Location: Pipersville, Pennsylvania.

c) The same fine barn, showing the wagon doors at the upper level. The barn appears to be greatly reduced in size from the façade in front, probably because of the simplicity of its elements, a pair of doors between two

walls. Also to be taken into account is the fact that the bottom half of the barn is below the upper level of the bank.
Location: same as *a*.

d) A pleasing pattern on a frame wall of circular ventilators. The doors when opened were used for winnowing or allowing straw to be dropped below after threshing. The roof is slate. The stone-enclosed farm-yard is often seen in Pennsylvania.
Location: R.R. 5, Carlisle, Pennsylvania.

a

b

era, it continued to be the access to the barn at the upper level, and is now used for the unloading of wheat or hay. When the harvest season is over, it serves as storage space for implements and vehicles, and there they remain throughout the winter.

The granary is basically a series of small rooms designed to hold the grain, the number being dependent on the size of the barn. As a rule they make few pretentions to architectural form, but one was found where the bins facing each other across the usual passage were given special treatment – in fact, a little arcade of three arches. The wagon doors were ordinarily set at grade level on the hilltop, but where that is not practical because of difference in grade, a gently sloping ramp provides a means of approach for the heavy laden wagons.

Depending on the size of the farm, the barn might have one, two, or even three threshing floors, each with its own pair of doors reaching to the eaves. As that might be twelve to sixteen feet high, the doors are necessarily massive and hung with strap hinges forged often on the farm and splendid examples of the iron worker's craft. Sur-

prising, because of its usefulness, is the comparative rarity outside of Quebec of the "guichet," or man-sized door let into one of the main doors. It is found in Pennsylvania and Ontario, and may best be recognized as the biblical "eye of a needle."

The illustration on this page shows how much goes on in a great barn. It is a Pennsylvania barn just outside the suburbs of Toronto, and while it has seen better days in a century and a quarter of active life, it is still a noble structure. Each department is marked on the plan, and it may be a surprise to many to see how varied were the functions that were accommodated within its four walls. The barn always was a building designed to house cattle, horses, pigs, calves, sometimes sheep, and the fodder to keep them alive over the winter. It knew a time when the animals were the source of food for the farmer and his family, and horses and oxen provided the motive power for all the heavier chores. It has been estimated that mechanization supplanted the patient ox in the years between 1900 and 1925, which in terms of agricultural or even human history is very recent.

Our old barn has therefore become something of an anachronism, and the threshing floor the depository of every kind of mechanized implement. Two threshing floors have once resounded to the beating of flails, and give an indication of the affluence the farm enjoyed in its heyday.

These are the elements which divide the space in the mow, but very significant for the reader who has read, or has yet to read the story of the Dutch barn, is the existence in this barn of that extremely ancient plan form, the nave with flanking aisles. One writer refers to these quite generous aisles as "galleries," and the term is a good one. With the nave they embody all the elements of the basilican plan. The astonishing thing is that visual separation is achieved by such simple means as posts in a rhythmic pattern of bays. It is true they are fine timbers – 12" x 12" and 18 feet high to the purlin in the roof slope, but they are still wood posts unadorned, except for the marks of the carpenter's adze. In looking at the framing of a barn like this we are looking at an achievement in vernacular architecture that can hardly be surpassed in any country. It is a structural system referred to elsewhere in this book and

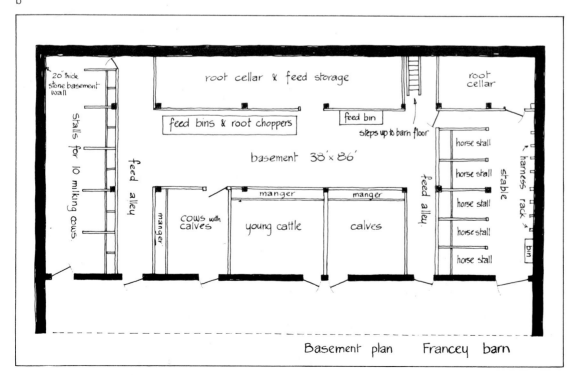

Basement plan Francey barn

a) Smaller than usual is the "eye of the needle" in the wagon door.
Location: near Ayton, Ontario.

b) Interior showing construction of a log barn in Pennsylvania built a hundred years before the barn shown in *d*. The importance of the comparison is the transference of a technique from log construction in Pennsylvania to frame in Ontario.

c

d

seen at its best in tithe barns like Great Coxwell in Britain. It is to be seen there and the rest of Europe in greater and smaller barns, but is found in North America only in the banked barn and Dutch barns, and, spectacularly, in the larger circular and polygonal barns.

The southerly aisle or gallery in the mow forms the ceiling of the forebay, the construction of which is extremely simple. In modern engineering terms, it is a cantilever formed by projecting the upper floor beyond the stable wall and supporting it by beams of quite extraordinary dimensions. Usually, they are spaced at three feet centres and consist of single timbers spanning the entire width of the barn. They receive support at two points – a sill at level of the base of the upper doors and the masonry or log wall at the rear of the forebay. In a barn of which mention shall be made again, beams were fifty feet long, and one monster still with its bark on two sides was twenty inches wide. Such a powerful cantilever was more than adequate to support the front wall of the gallery in clapboard or vertical siding, as well as taking its share of the load of timber framing and the roof.

As the nineteenth century advanced and the forest receded, timbers on the heroic scale of the ones mentioned above disappeared entirely. Barns are found, no less handsome than their predecessors, where the lightness of the beams called for a plate to hold their ends and stone, or concrete columns or posts to support the plate. The shelter remained, but the cantilever as a structural form had departed.[8]

There are banked barns without a forebay, but the idea of protection was there – if not for the cattle, at least for the wall, doors and windows of the stable wall. This was achieved by a "pent" or "pentice" which was really a lean-to roof of limited projection, but long enough to protect the entire wall. "Pentice" is an old English word not found in ordinary dictionaries, but it refers to just this kind of canopy and its use, and is usually restricted to barns.[9] Its projection would rarely exceed two feet.

For obvious reasons, the front wall of the mow was always of wood, and there are many fine Pennsylvania barns that, including the stable, cow byre wall, which takes most of the load of the forebay, are built entirely of wood. Writing in 1955, Alfred Shoemaker could say that "today, the vast majority of Pennsylvania barns are frame."[10] The 1798 direct tax returns show that at that date Pennsylvania was overwhelmingly a state of log or cabin barns.[11] The same records state that in the entire state there were only ten brick barns, and stone barns were limited to the hills and valleys to the southeast. "Frame barns," says Shoemaker, "were a relative rarity in the eighteenth century."[12] It says much for the durable qualities of white pine that barns built in the early years of the nineteenth century still stand. They are recognized by their narrow tapered boards—slightly concave, it is true, and worn by sun, rain, and frost to a thickness that looks, and often is, fragile to the touch. The same is true of ancient cedar shingles on the barn wall. It is usually impossible to date a barn, and happy are they who find a name and a date carved in wood or stone.

Fortunately it is possible to give dates to two barns of wood, even to the stable walls, in the Toronto area, and they are illustrated in these pages. One is the Dalziel barn (1809) and the other, the Baker barn,

c) The Francey, Ontario barn again (89d), this time showing one of the posts that separate the "aisle" from the "nave."

d) Another view of the Francey barn, looking very much like the skeleton of a wooden ship. Five tie beams can be seen, each one supporting two inclined purlin posts with their braces forming a fan. Such a framed structure provided ample open space for loading hay.

a

b

a) Byre wall of log in the Baker barn. The low wall of large boulders and shallow stones would be admired by the Japanese, who would also hold in high regard this masterpiece of 1822 in timber construction. Location: see 87b.

b) The barn itself. The roof is a gabled hip and the forebay is partly protected by the end wall. In very old Ontario barns, clapboard was used as early as 1809. Vertical boarding was the common sheathing in Pennsylvania. The interior is log crib construction. Location: see 87b.

c

d

e

c) A barn famous for its size (it is almost a square in plan) and for its reputed distinguished designer, Sir Casimir Gzowski. The building did not lack ventilation from louvres, light from charming windows, or heat from a fire in the stable. The flue in the thickness of the wall emerges as a small chimney at the peak of the gable.
Location: Rockwood, Ontario.

d) Very rare indeed is a parapet on a gable, a device often seen on houses in the Cotswolds in England and elsewhere, but not on barns in North America. The illustration shows its termination at the eave.
Location: same as c.

e) The other gable end. The chimney is clearly visible.
Location: same as c.

a

is undoubtedly 1822.

Outstanding among barns for the excellence of their carpentry are the Pennsylvania barn, the English, and the Dutch barns of New York State. In one typical Ontario Pennsylvania example, all wood members were precut and numbered: posts and beams, purlins and rafters were adzed, but where carpentry approached the level of joinery, as it did in the shaping of mortice and tenons, the timber was sawn. Holes were bored in the pine logs and oak pegs locked the members in place. Nails, however admirably they might be forged, were forbidden. As someone said, prefabrication was elevated to a science before the term was even invented, and erection of the framework awaited only the arrival of friends and neighbours and the gift of a fine day.

So long as there is a forebay and a hillside, the long façade will be in frame construction. So might the gable ends, but for the traveller in Pennsylvania, his happiest memories will be of gable walls in brick or stone. They are the really great barns of the state. Sketches show two different treatments for these end

a) As the forests receded and the massive timbers necessary to support the mow over the forebay became unavailable, lighter beams were substituted. They terminated in a plate, which was supported, as we see here, on sturdy stone columns. This new support produced at times a deeper forebay.
Location: Young's Road. Chester County, Pennsylvania.

b) The barn nestles comfortably into the hill, where at the top it is only one storey high. In this case, the columns supporting the forebay are tapered, and constructed of rubble set in mortar and plastered for weather protection.
Location: near West Chester County, Pennsylvania.

b

d

c) A little cloistered court in a ∩-shaped barn near Woodstock, Ontario.

d) Less substantial supports on an Ontario barn. There is a forebay, but the wagon doors above would indicate that in its prime this was an English barn, which a later generation raised to a new foundation. Location: Varney, Ontario.

c

a

b

c

a) This banked barn is one of the most attractive barns in Ontario. The masonry is superb (Scottish masons) and keystones are formed by a sheaf of wheat in relief. The upper door serves the threshing floor.
Location: Elora, Ontario.

b) The stone Pennsylvania barn at its rugged best. An arcade takes the place of columns supporting the forebay, obviously necessary because the superstructure is stone and not wood.
Location: near Sellersville, Pennsylvania.

c) Really great architecture which may be compared with vernacular building in any country. This barn belongs to a type known as "three-decker," with (a) animals at the lowest level, (b) granary above, and (c) the threshing floor.
Location: Birmingham Road, Chester County, Pennsylvania.

b

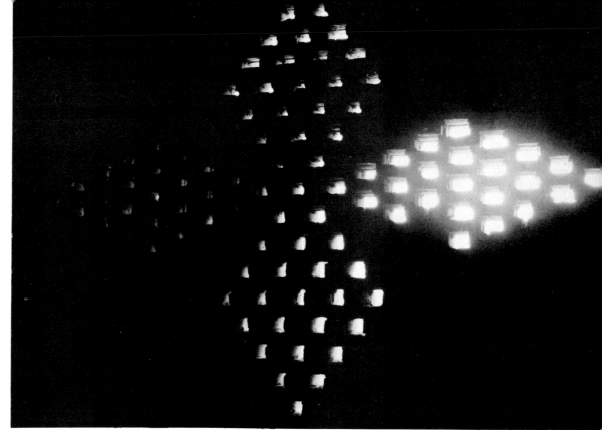

c

d

e

a) Interior of a brick barn, showing the framing of a bent and the delightful pattern of light through the brick openings.
Location: near East Berlin, Pennsylvania, on Route 194.

b) The spectacular effect of the rider on his ass from inside the barn.
Location: near Greencastle, Pennsylvania, on Route 16.

c) The starburst in the barn in a.

d) This barn is famous for the tale attached to the mule in the gable. The story goes that the owner desired a riding horse, but, after an acrimonious dispute with his master bricklayer, he departed for a period of several days. In his absence, the bricklayer substituted a man on an ass for the owner on his riding horse, with results that can be imagined.
Location: near Greencastle, Pennsylvania, on Route 16.

e) Brick ventilating openings in a stone wall.

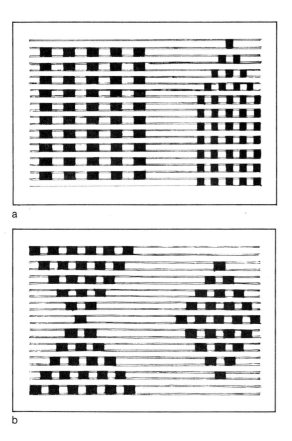

a

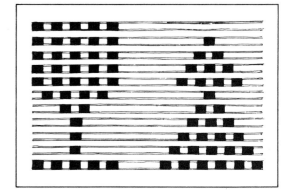

c

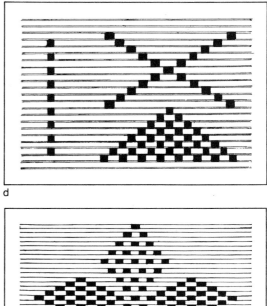

d

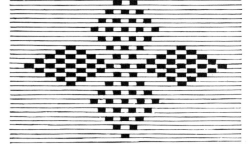

b

e

walls—one, where the frame construction over the forebay is frankly exposed in clapboard, and, two, where the brick of the gable is carried out to enclose the forebay and the mow above.

These gable ends get their charm from the excellence of the brickwork, but more particularly from the ingenuity with which the old masons turned the need for ventilation in the mow into patterns of great beauty by the simple device of omitting bricks. The patterns may take any number of forms ranging from a rectangle to a goblet, or, very daringly, a series of gothic windows. What the visitor does not realize till shown is that these patterns, while delightful externally, are spectacular and luminous when seen from inside the barn. Henry Glassie points out that "this form of decorative brick construction was employed as early as the fifteenth century on barns in England, notably in the counties of Staffordshire, Cheshire and Shropshire.[13] It was brought by the English to eastern Virginia and carried from the Tidewater into northern Georgia and Kentucky; in all of these southern areas its use was restricted to small out buildings. It was certainly introduced in Pennsylvania by the English and it is interesting to note that one of the most characteristic elements of Pennsylvania German folk architecture has an English provenance."[14]

William Stair, writing in 1955, was of the opinion that the brick end barns extant were not so very old: "The early part of the previous century (1750–1850) saw few barns of this kind constructed since the period was one of uncertainty to the farmer, and barns therefore were smaller and built of logs, of wooden boards, or occasionally of stone."

The manufacture of bricks was a growing commercial enterprise by the second half of the nineteenth century, but in many cases the clay on the farm was suitable for brick making, and the itinerant bricklayer made the bricks on the spot. And to carry the process a step further, it was not unknown when limestone was available for it to be burned in kilns, and the lime made ready for mortar. Walls are frequently sixteen inches thick, and failure is practically unknown in spite of elaborate piercing for ventilation. Bricks followed the standard American dimension of 2¼" x 3¾" x 8", but in early barns an oversized brick 2½" x 4½" x 9¼" was put to

use.[15] Bond, or the setting up of bricks in their rows, adds greatly to the interest and structural stability of a wall, even if it is a hefty sixteen inches thick. There are many types of bond, but in Pennsylvania we find two good standbys: common or English bond, where every sixth course is a row of headers, and Flemish, in which header bricks follow stretchers in every course.

a–e) Various patterns of openings in brickwork: *a* is the "square" or "bushel measure" and "gothic window"; *b*, the "sheaf of wheat" and "diamond"; *c*, the "wineglass" and "Christmas tree"; *d*, the "vertical slot", simple "X", and triangle; and *e*, the unfolding lily.

f

f) Detail of gable showing ventilation openings.
Location: see g.

g) This barn was built in 1861, and may represent the
last word in the bricklayer's art. The arched opening at
the right-hand corner is occasionally found in this
location and its use varied with different barns.
Location: near McAllisterville, Juniata County,
Pennsylvania.

g

a

b

c

d

e

a) Stable door.
Location: Green Valley Road, Chester County, Pennsylvania.

b) A fine design, in which the stable doors and two small windows contrast with an area of uninterrupted masonry. Vernacular architecture at its best.
Location: same as *a*.

c) A porch with wagon doors forms a bridge between the head of the ramp and the barn. Under it is the

entrance to the granary and space for storage of implements. Flanking the entrance are slatted corn cribs.
Location: same as *a*.

d) An interesting gable, showing how over the small one-level English barn another generation added a three-decker banked barn. Datestone, 1767.
Location: near Marlborough, Chester County, Pennsylvania.

e) Beauty in stone—a serpentine green stone wall
Location: near West Chester, Pennsylvania.

f) There is a definite appeal to the viewer in the great Pennsylvania barn in its simple basic form—no fine brickwork, no colourful hexes, no embellishment like a cupola. It just stands there, the veteran of over a century of harvests and weather in all its moods.
Location: off Route 219, Somerset County, Pennsylvania.

g) A stone barn with forebay frankly expressed. The alternative will be seen where the end walls in stone or brick form an end to the projecting mow.
Location: near Schaefferstown, Pennsylvania.

f

g

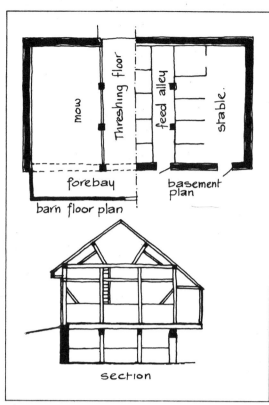

mow

Threshing floor

feed alley

stable.

forebay

barn floor plan

basement plan

section

a,b

One can still travel over a good deal of Pennsylvania country without coming across a stone or stone end barn. Mr. Shoemaker has shown that what was demonstrated in the tax records of 1798 is also true today – the range of the stone barns is limited to the southeastern part of the state. His reason for the impression of early travellers that the state was one of stone barns was the fact that their route in those days lay between Philadelphia and Harrisburg or between Boston and Harrisburg – or vice versa. Those are the trails we must follow today, and nothing can be more rewarding than the sight of a great Pennsylvania stone barn.

What is evident in the following pages is that whatever its origins, and they were various, the Pennsylvania barn of today is a wholly American creation, and is a structure that may rank with the most distinguished vernacular architecture of any country in the world.

The Pennsylvania barn could be summarized as follows:

Name:
It is strictly a banked barn, but because of the examples in Pennsylvania, and its origin in that state, it is frequently known as the Pennsylvania barn. It is found elsewhere, but even in Ontario the few samples that exist are known locally as Pennsylvania barns.

Site:
(a) Almost always it is built into a hill of sufficient height to permit the mow floor to be level with the hill top. Failing that, a ramp—often the width of the barn—will provide an approach for wagons to the mow floor. (b) A favourable aspect for the barn is south so that advantage may be taken of the forebay for sheltering cattle in suitable weather. (c) The long axis of the barn runs with the lie of the hill, or east-west if (b) applies.

Use:
The barn is designed for livestock on the ground floor, and implement storage and the storage of hay, unthreshed grain and the grain itself in the granary on the second.

Plan:
The barn at ground level is not remarkable for the disposition of departments; cattle, horses, sheep, pigs are fairly standard in all

barns, but the sheltered space in front formed by the forebay is unique and not found in other barn types. Because of its location on the bank side, this space permitted frost-free storage of root crops such as turnips. Another feature, which the banked barn shares with the Dutch barn of New York State, is the division of the mow floor into galleries (aisles) and central space (nave). This division, an architectural feature of great significance, is formed by massive posts forming bays.

Section:
(a) The forebay is the characteristic feature of the banked barn and is formed by the extension of the mow floor as a cantilever on which rests the south part of the mow. In such a case, the beams at 3′0″ centres forming the cantilever receive support at the upper door sill and the livestock wall, which may be built of timber or stone. These are massive beams and belong to the days of virgin forest and the availability of great timbers. (b) In later times, such beams were not to be had, and in order to preserve the overhang and the shelter it provided, an east-west beam supported the mow wall and rested on stone or concrete columns, or wooden posts.
(c) There are banked barns without a forebay; i.e. the livestock wall and the mow are in one vertical plane. The need or the desire to protect the windows and doors in the lower part of the wall produced the "pentice"–a lean-to roof of 2:3 feet projection. The same pentice is sometimes found over the wagon doors on the upper level. (d) Rather uncommon are banked barns with negligible (10-12 inches) overhang of the mow as protection for the wall below, reminiscent of barns or houses similarly treated in Europe.

Materials:
The south front of the mow is universally of wood frame construction, as the load on the cantilever precludes the use of stone or brick. Adzed logs are sometimes found to form the livestock wall at the rear of the forebay, but more often it is masonry. Roofs are covered with shingle, slate or metal. The end walls (rarely clapboard) are best known for the beauty of brickwork, stone, or stone with brick openings. It is in these end walls that the old masons had such fun devising panels of various shapes, omitting bricks, to provide ventilation.

a,b) Plan and section of a typical Pennsylvania-type barn.

c) A Pennsylvania barn with matching ventilating chimneys and embrasures on all sides. The flues in the chimneys took stale air away from the stables and are not to be confused with the one at Rockwood, Ontario, which took smoke from a burning stove.

d) Primitive masonry suggesting an entrance to a pre-historic cave. Actually, a turnip chute to the root cellar in the basement which was capable of holding 300 bushels of mangels. The root cellar measured 50′ x 40′. Location: near Eramosa, Ontario.

e) The gable shows ventilation by slits for the mow and by a flue for the stable—enjoyed by the pigeon.

c

d

e

a

c

b

d

e

a) This is a fine example of an Ontario barn used in its day to house great crops. To give an idea of its dimensions, the centre is 98′ by 72′ and the wings are each 54′ long. In the two pictures we see the barn in summer and in winter.
Location: near Ayton, Grey County, Ontario.

b) The same barn, proud and confident on its hilltop site.

c) A magnificent example of the banked barn on the Laurentian Shield. The vast expanse of cedar shingle bears down on a series of wood posts supporting the forebay.
Location: Calabogie, Ontario.

d) A stone barn given a salt box silhouette by an addition at the lower level. The date-stone gives 1847 as the time of building of the original barn.
Location: Crewson's Corners, Ontario.

e) The red and black barns never look so well as against a foreground of snow. This silhouette is often seen in Ontario–the low wing is usually referred to as the straw barn.
Location: near Highway 10, Ontario.

g

h

f

k

j

l

f) Stone barn with pentice and walled yard.
Location: Radnor, Pennsylvania.

g) A popular barn type with typical stone stable walls, and not so common, the stone ends that enclose the forebay.
Location: near Huff's Church, Berks County, Pennsylvania.

h) This fine barn is now the Kempton Farm Museum.
Location: Kempton, Pennsylvania.

j) Illustrated here just for gorgeous colour and simplicity of form.
Location: near East Winfield, N.Y.

k) An Upper-New-York-State adaptation of the banked barn.
Location: Route 104 near Lockport, New York.

l) A late expression of the banked barn in Quebec, with hipped roof and, on the left, the ramp to the hay mow.
Location: St.-Gervais, Quebec

a

b

c

a) See 108a.

b) What we see to the right of the post and the stacked hay is a major extension. The structural solution was the great struts getting support from posts in the outside wall.
Location: same as a.

c) A spectacular view showing the massive hewn timber or central post in the bent with ladder attached.
Location: same as a.

d) Beauty of space, structural ingenuity, craftsmanship and light.
Location: same as a.

d

a

a) Even at the height of the industrial revolution of the nineteenth century, mass-produced hardware had not reached the farm. Like the craftsman in the Middle Ages, the farmer got happiness in making things that today are bought from a catalogue. He could use wood or metal, or, as in this illustration, a combination of the two. It was part of the philosophy of William Morris that real joy in creation came from the combination of designing and ''doing,'' and we see here and else-where in these pages what inventive farmers brought to the making of a bolt and latch.

b) Another handsome all-wood "door set," fitting so perfectly into its background of smooth wide brown boards.

b

a

The Quebec Connected Barn

Chapter 4

b

c

There can be few countries in the world that have in their archives legal descriptions of their barns of the seventeenth century, their shape, materials, quality of workmanship and other details, and, while less precise, enough records from the sixteenth century to give us, with a little imagination, a fair idea of their appearance. These records are preserved in the archives of the Province of Quebec. This chapter is concerned with connected barns in Quebec, the *maison bloc* of Brittany, but it will be postponed briefly for readers unfamiliar with early agricultural experiments in Canada, which were not without influence on the evolution of the barn in the New World.

To begin with, there was Jacques Cartier (1491–1557), who in 1541 with twenty men at work prepared an acre and a half of ground for cabbages, turnips and lettuce, probably at Cap Rouge nine miles above Quebec. The first Canadian farmer was Louis Hébert, who grew grains and vegetables near Quebec in 1615. For thirteen years, his family must have farmed entirely by the labour of their hands and the sturdiness of their backs, for it was not until 1628 that a son-in-law in France sent them a wooden plough. They waited until 1647 for their first sight of a horse.

An important settlement in those early days was established by French Jesuit priests on the shores of the Georgian Bay near the modern Ontario town of Midland. It was known as the Mission of Ste. Marie to the Hurons, and later as Fort Ste. Marie, a palisaded structure that served as a retreat for the Fathers, and as a place with some semblance of defence in case of attack. The journey from Quebec was one of incredible difficulty – eight hundred miles were covered, and the impedimenta of the priests included primitive farm implements, seed for the cereal crops and grapes they intended to grow at the mission, and a few cattle. The experiment was successful, and included barley and oats as well as native crops of corn and sunflowers, but the mission ended disastrously in the destruction of all the buildings and the death by torture of the Fathers Lalement and Brébeuf.

The buildings have been reconstructed on the old foundations, and great pains have been taken in using the construction methods of seventeenth-century France, along with the materials available to the

a) The Behrer barn. (See 123*d*.)

b) A remarkable reconstruction of the Jesuit Mission of Ste.-Marie-among-the-Hurons near Midland, Ontario. Pains have been taken to use the construction methods that would have been known to the Fathers in 1639.

c) The stable, showing "palisade" construction and the beautiful roof, formed by shingles of elm bark. Everything was destroyed in 1649.
Location: near Midland, Ontario.

a

a) Typical of the Quebec long barn, in many ways, is
this one with the low eave broken only by the hay door
in the dormer. Typical, too, of many in this part of
Quebec is the barn built close to the road.
Location: Château Richer, Quebec.

b) A cradle scythe hangs beneath the eave.

b

116

c

Fathers in the forest wilderness of 1638.

Another seventeenth-century attempt to carve a home out of the forest took place in 1676 at Fort Frontenac, the site of the modern city of Kingston, Ontario. This also was a Jesuit Mission, under the direction of Father Hennepin, later to be remembered as the first white man to see Niagara Falls. His was a major agricultural experiment, as he is reported to have brought over a hundred acres under cultivation, and that part of the wilderness saw for the first time European as well as Indian corn, pulse,¹ barley, gourds and watermelons.

These settlements in the primeval forest were far from the nerve centre of New France, *l'habitation* at Quebec. As early as 1626, life was so crowded within its walls that pasture had to be found elsewhere. In that year, Champlain chose Cap Tourmente for the new settlement, a satellite town of village dimensions for which the first requirements were buildings to protect the animals against the rigours of the Quebec winter, and to provide storage for hay. The first horse, as has been mentioned, did not arrive until 1647, but the cows were there and, as beasts of

burden on the farm, there would be oxen.

Champlain's specifications for the stable were that it be "60 feet long and 20 feet wide - made of wood and earth, like those in the villages of Normandy." There were, in addition, two little barns of the same construction. This establishment was the prototype of many succeeding barns in the province, and it is interesting to have a clue from Champlain himself as to their origin. Frequent in old provincial records is a reference to *"gasparde,"* which was a time-honoured construction for a wall all over Europe – none other than cob or wattle and daub, the network of sticks used as a bond for mud or plaster that appears so often in these pages.

The plan arrangements of the Quebec farmstead fall into two categories as they did in old France, the *maison cour* and the *maison bloc*. The former consisted of separate and distinct farm buildings grouped about a court, and was the traditional layout of the homestead in Normandy, and the latter was a connected barn, which in the homeland was usually the establishment of a poor or tenant farmer, and consisted of house, barn, cattle shed and any other outbuilding gathered under one unbroken roof. This was the traditional layout of the small Breton farmstead.

The long stone Breton farm buildings with their thatched roofs frankly declare the identity of their different parts. The house part with its windows and entrance door suggests a welcome, while other doors and windows on a different scale proclaim the presence of cattle or the implements within. An almost universal feature in such a building was the dormer door, which admitted hay or sheaves at harvest time and stood at eave level or a little below, close to the house part. It was reached in some of the more substantial examples by a solid stone stair usually without handrails, or, simply, by a ladder. The mow, if it may be so called, was filled by hand because the stair effectively prevented the backing up of trucks and the forking of sheaves through the dormer door. A small statue of the Virgin Mary often appears to one side of the head of steps, obviously with the thought of a benediction – a blessing of the harvest. A cross is usual on the gables of the *horreos* or granaries of Spain, and the figure of the Christ in a niche over a barn door in Quebec was a happy discovery.

d

e

c) A Quebec bull with what must surely be a headdress of medieval origin.

d) A *horreo* (or granary) in Galicia. The cross in the gable end is frequently found in barns in Catholic communities.

e) Statuette of Christ in a niche on a barn in Quebec. Delightful in itself and unexpected, it suggests, like the cross, the blessings of the church on livestock and crops, and also a continuity of ownership in the family of the farmer.
Location: Château Richer.

a

b

a) A barn overlooking the St. Lawrence River in which
we see many characteristics of the barn in Quebec.
The doors and windows tell their own story of storage
and cattle and the hay door which serves the loft over
the cows. Note should be made of the low eave and
the slightly undulating unbroken ridge to the roof.
Location: St.-Pierre, Ile d'Orléans.

b) A hay cart.

c

d

It was on this Breton model that the *maison bloc* had its origin in Quebec in the seventeenth century. Two such farmsteads now converted to domestic use have been photographed on the Ile d'Orléans. What is important is that even without the *maison* the Breton form remained in the great nineteenth-century barns. The dormer evolved as a dominating and striking element in the façade, and served as a wagon entrance to the left over the stable.

In the notaries' documents already referred to, records are given of forty-seven barns erected in the region of Quebec, Montreal and Three Rivers during the period 1662–1771.[2] A few, taken at random, tell the story of the connected barn in Quebec, some of them during the reign of Louis XIV. In 1694, the merchant Pierre Renthuys rented "half a stable which he added to the end of his house on Notre Dame Street [Montreal] to winter his animals." In an inventory of 1703, it is recorded that "in the barn which is joined to the above mentioned house, the aforesaid Langevin and his wife claim to have seven hundred and fifty sheaves of wheat," and in the stable adjoining the said house, forty five cattle lodged under the same roof as the Hurtebise family.

As a final example, there is the story of the master mason and stone cutter Jean-Baptiste Deguire who contracted to build a house at the corner of Notre Dame and St. Gabriel Street in Montreal. The building was to measure 48′ x 30′ with a horse stable at the end measuring 16′ x 10′–a mite of a stable, as these were outside dimensions.

Even at a very early date, barn-cum-byre structures made their appearance without a house attached. These are important in a discussion of the connected barn because they are the forerunners of the splendid one-storey nineteenth-century barns which are illustrated in the following pages.

1. December 29, 1703. Paul le Moine de Maricourt had among his possessions "a barn with attached sheds serving as a stable, 78 feet long and 20 feet wide made of stakes with a plank roof."[3]

2. February 15, 1734. The property of Jean Poupart, of Saint Lambert, includes "a barn, and a stable at the said barn of hewn log construction, *pièce sur pièce* [logs laid horizontally] and roofed with straw."[4]

3. February 1759. The heirs of Jacques

c) This is one of the few remaining *maison bloc* farmsteads in which, at one time, the family shared the building with livestock. It has since been converted to residential use.
Location: Ile d'Orléans, Montmorency County.

d) Like the illustration above, this was a *maison bloc* farmstead and, we might assume, the central opening once led to the threshing floor.
Location: Ile d'Orléans.

a

a) This is the Quebec connected barn par excellence.
Doors to the threshing floors and lesser door for cattle
all declare themselves in the façade.
Location: Rue Notre Dame, near Ancienne-Lorette.

b

c

d

b) The old barn of M. Hector Gravel is interesting for its log walling and the use of "storm" doors, which are often a feature of the Quebec barn. The remains of the buggy and the clusters of onions beneath the eave complete the scene.
Location: St.-Jean-Baptiste, Charlevoix.

c) A delightful detail in which windows and white-washed planked wall seem to give focus to the stable door and beautifully modelled little horse.
Location: Neuville, Portneuf County.

d) An example of a barn with a hipped roof, not common in North America.
Location: near St.-Pierre, Ile d'Orléans.

a

b

c

Painiey owned at Chambly a twenty-foot barn with walls of posts set in the ground and roofed with straw, and a stable at the end of the same barn.[5]

The tendency to divorce the house from the barn continued until, in the nineteenth century, few farmsteads remained where house and barn were one. Nevertheless, the quality, the lowness and the long eave line of the *maison bloc* were retained in a new combination of barn, stable, byre, and implement shed. Only the *maison* was missing.

Two materials only were available to the settlers for walls, and they were stone and wood. The visitor to Quebec will come away with a memory of charming stone houses where the masonry was of a kind he had seen only in Europe – a masonry where the mortar was "laid on with a trowel," an expression that is usually uncomplimentary. The mortar is generous on such Quebec houses, but it is deliberately and skilfully done. Many an immigrant farmer with a love of stone and knowledge of its use would bitterly regret using it in the early days in Quebec. Unfortunately, he was a century or two away from modern waterproofing materials, and the

stone barn could mean disaster for him. R. L. Séguin quotes from the writings of Mother Françoise Juchereau, who had ordered the construction of a stable for the Hotel Dieu in the summer of 1691: "We had built a stable of stone in which to winter the animals. However, we discovered by experience that nothing is less appropriate for this purpose than stone buildings because of an accumulation of hoar frost that forms on the walls and causes an unhealthy chill in the animals. It would have been better in wood, it would have cost less, the repairs might have been less and we would have lodged our cattle more warmly in winter." Wood was clearly the answer to the settlers problems and it was used in a variety of ways perhaps best understood in tabulated form:

The walls
Pièce sur pièce
The barn was divided into bays marked by posts with the space between filled in with heavy planks or squared logs. The posts were slotted throughout their height and the plank ends were so shaped as to fit into the vertical slot. The wall post construction was

a) Shrinkage shows how the logs are slotted in a vertical channel into the uprights. The pretty pine spray was blessed by the priest and placed there by ancient custom on Palm Sunday. Protection is sought for the barn against lightning.
Location: St.-Urbain.

b) Thatch and the frank display of rods that were part of the indigenous technique of thatch-laying.

c) Another example of solid log construction, in which the dressed logs are not merely lying one on the other but are structurally integral with the post–*pièce sur pièce*. With this construction, bays could be added right and left to the barn when needed. This was a merit not found in the log barn with dovetailed corners, which was finite in conception.

d

known as *pièce sur pièce* or *en coulisse* to indicate the locking into the posts.

Sheathing
Less substantial than the *pièce sur pièce* was the use of overlapping heavy planks without taper over studs. Half logs with the bark on the outside were spiked to uprights (heavy studs) as sheathing–much like planks.

Palisade
Vertical posts or stakes were driven into the ground or set on a sill to avoid damp.

Roof
Thatch
Early roofs were of thatch, a technique familiar to the immigrant, but what was available, straw or "ocean hay," was inferior to the old country reed thatch and tended to become soggy. There are still thatched barns in Quebec, but the itinerant thatcher and his craft have long since disappeared.

Plank
Overlapping planks of unbelievable dimensions were used. On the barn for Lambert

d) This truly great barn was photographed in the year 1900, and what it looks like today is shown on the following page. It may be nearly two hundred years old. It is known in Quebec as the Behrer barn after its builder, a farmer with a German background. The overhanging mow serves no purpose in terms of gained space, and could have been the result of nostalgic memories of home or a practical desire to protect the doors below. The ridge shows very well the crossed-log system of holding down the thatch. Location: Cap l'Aigle.

a

b

c

e

d

f

a) Notched log construction. The labour of flattening or dressing the face of the logs was here thought worthwhile by the carpenter.
Location: Charlevoix County.

b) The Behrer barn seventy years later. The inevitable change was from ''hay'' thatch to watertight cedar shingles and whitewashed walls. See 123c and frontispiece to this chapter.

c) Often painted by artists is this barn with separate ramps to the two dormers which have a powerful influence on the design.
Location: east of St.-Charles, Bellechasse County.

d) The simple and effective framing of the barn in c. The heavy rafters are half lapped and pegged, and covered by thick, tight-fitting roof boards that add to the stability of the barn.

e) This little barn in undeniably French from its whitewashed walls to its steep roof. Two minor items of the roof are worth a note: the extension of the ridge to take a pulley and the flue pipe on the right that ventilates the stable.

f) Higher ground gives better approach to the wagon doors and the mow.
Location: near St.-Pierre, Montmagny County.

a

b

c

Closse (Montreal, 1662) it was specified that no "iron ware" was to be used, though roof planks were 5″–6″ thick. Heavy planks disappeared with the retreat of the forests, but handsplit shingles were an admirable substitute.

General

From the notaries' documents, much can be learned about the settlers' choice of woods for different functions, like the threshing floor which was built to take the pounding of the flail and was usually 5″–6″ thick and made of oak or cedar. Rafters were of oak, and framing was generally done in oak, walnut, ash, hemlock, basswood or pine. Major beams were basswood or hemlock, and the same were specified for the heavy planks in walls. The squared logs or *pièce sur pièce* walls, posts and stakes were cedar. The sill at ground level or on low stone piers was almost always hemlock.

The following reconstruction of a typical barn of 1711 is taken from the notary's description of one for M. Pierre Gadois, with a few items from other barns to complete the picture.

A. The barn was to be 30 feet by 22 feet.

B. Construction, *pièce sur pièce* of any wood except for the sills which will be walnut or pine (hemlock not mentioned here for sills).

C. Height to the eaves to be 10 feet. (Carré).

D. Roof, *faîte sur faîte* with braces, tie beams, and rafters. (Rafters were usually oak, trimmed on four sides and on three-foot centres but sometimes were untrimmed poles). *Faîte sur faîte* is uniquely French Canadian and refers to a heavy beam (longitudinal in the barn) a few feet below the "roof tree" or ridge board.

E. Gables to be colombage construction to take planks or thatch. (In a barn of 1685, the roofing material was described as grass.) Frequently, as at the barn of le Sieur de Villenay, 1682, the contractor "will make two crosses of St. Andrew *(deux crois de St. André)*" which were trusses in wood forming such a cross. "Columbage" is a Norman term for half-timbered construction. It can also de-

scribe a row of upright posts in a partition.

F. The threshing floor to be 10 feet wide and the timbers laid across the floor 4 inches thick of the choicest wood which the contractor will find in the cedar patch of the said Gadois. If, however, the timber there is not sufficiently good, he will construct the said threshing floor of white wood (basswood) of squared timbers 4 inches thick.

We get an indication of the interior arrangement of an early barn from a drawing of M. Séguin's. It is a small barn and unattached to house or byre. It is just longer than a square, and is divided into three sections, the centre being the threshing floor flanked by grain bins. On one side sheaves are stored waiting to be threshed, and on the other, hay. The single entrance would take the door in two leaves, one with the little "guichet." It is surprising that there was not another door to the threshing floor to provide the draft for separating the grain from the chaff, and to make backing out unnecessary.

G. (From the barn of Pierre Penthuys, who rented a barn at Pointe au Trembles in 1694.) The walls of the grain bins, one on each side of the threshing floor, to be 20 or 22 inches high and made up of squared cedar logs morticed into the door posts.

H. The door to be 10 feet high and 10 feet wide and "at least 7 inches thick." It will be a single door with *un petit guichet*. As the little door was to be fitted with strap hinges, it is presumed to be one of a size just big enough to admit a man. (Such doors are not uncommon in the Province.) Only the word "Judas" describes a spy hole or slit in a door. Séguin cites two examples of barn doors (1684 and 1698) for which the contractor was to supply locks.

I. A curious note in the specification for the Gadois barn states it was to be paid for with blacksmith's tools! – anvil, two hammers, tongs, bellows, files, etc.

The reader will get the impression that the barns mentioned of the seventeenth and eighteenth centuries were small. On the average, they were 30 feet by 20 feet, and some might reach 50 or 60 feet in length. Even so, M. Séguin points out that they were

a) Here is a trio of doors on which the builder lavished a good deal of affection. In addition to the Greek revival architrave which frames the doors, each of the vertical planks is divided by bead mould. It is a curious fact that barn doors like these open inward in Quebec, and out in Ontario and elsewhere in North America. Many advantages can be thought of for each method, though a fire marshal's preference would be for the door opening out.
Location: St.-Augustin.

b) An elliptical arch frames the wagon doors, and is repeated on the "guichet." Each arch has its own "keystone."
Location: L'Ange-Gardien.

c) A small log barn with "frieze" and roof of planks, an early sheathing for roofs now rarely seen. The square ends of timbers showing above the door are supports for the floor of the loft.
Location: St.-Jean-Baptiste, Charlevoix County.

generally larger than barns in France, and he gives as a reason that, as the frost in Canada comes earlier and stays later, the habitant had to count on one crop per year to feed his family and animals. When the Pierre Penthuys referred to above died in Montreal in 1708, he had four hundred bales of hay in his barn, and as this was in April, he must have had considerably more in the autumn.

In his valuable book *Les Granges du Québec,* M. R. L. Séguin shows barn plans with one and two threshing floors, each flanked by a grain bin and mow. In large barns built in the days of flail that for a century and more preceded the threshing machine in Quebec, two floors on one plane may have served a very useful purpose. In several venerable barns, areas are recognized that once knew the pounding of the flailer on a polished floor, but which in their old age serve merely as accommodation for implements, some of them as outdated as the space they fill. This suggests a flexibility in the plan arrangements of the old low barn that is not as easily achieved in the two-storey barn outside of Quebec where the single old threshing floor has to double as drive-in "shed" in late summer and implement storage in winter. The barn plans of M. Bibeau and M. Bherer show quite clearly which areas are now anachronistic and which still fulfil their ancient functions.

The Bibeau barn measures 125′ x 25′ and Bherer 90′ x 25′. Even seen in photograph, it will be agreed that their lowness gives an illusion of greater size. Compared with other barns of their period in Quebec, they are large, but tiny beside the great stone barn at New Lebanon (300 feet) or the St. Benoît barn with a diameter over 70 feet. Much that is typical of the Quebec barn is revealed in the illustrations of M. Goulet's barn at Lac St. Augustin. Taking first the walls, it will be noted that they are constructed of planks placed vertically and butted, and so marvellously seasoned and laid that, at a distance, they might appear to be smooth stucco. Examples of such precision are to be found, though rarely, in house architecture of early times in Canada and the United States, but nearly always the boards were tongued and grooved. There was nothing so fancy in this barn, and its date, set modestly in a gable over the wagon door, reads 1810. There is much to be admired in the walls, but it is

impossible to think of this barn without its magnificent roof.

The traveller in Quebec who has a weather eye for barns will be struck first of all by their lowness compared with anything to which he may be accustomed, and, secondly, by their roofs. The dark horizontality of the roof resting on white walls undoubtedly adds greatly to the visual effect of lowness. All the roof types of North America are to be seen in Quebec, and none seems inappropriate in its setting. Even the mansard, which for this observer is not a happy solution to the roofing problems of suburbia and some barns, is extraordinarily effective on the French Canadian barn. It can be seen sitting happily on the polygonal, and, now equally so on the barn of M. Goulet. In this case, the roof differs from the standard mansard section in that the lower part takes the form of a cove, a "kick" to the roof that even the great François Mansard would have approved. He would have expressed his satisfaction, too, with the three cupola ventilators on the ridge, and the tidy dormers that stand on the eave and give light to the mow. How beautiful, too, is the end of the barn where the white boards rise to the level of the upper slope of the mansard.

The hip predominates, but there are gabled hips, gables and hipped gables, and, later, in the procession of years, the gambrel for which Mr. Eric Sloane has a very novel interpretation not found in dictionaries. He shows a drawing of a gambrel, a shaped bar used by butchers, and if sloping sides are added to it, the gambrel roof form emerges. Its merit, especially for the storage of hay, is in its steep inside walls, unwasted floor space, and consequently greater cubic contents.

The hip in Quebec is sometimes of normal pitch, but more often steeply French and coved at the eave. The late Professor Nobbs of McGill University, who was an authority on French Canadian architecture, was of the opinion that the bell cast eave was an innovation not known in Brittany or Normandy and, structurally, a disaster for Quebec. In a tour of the province, he showed this writer many examples where snow had melted, and, by capillary action, drawn water under the shingles which then penetrated the house. Water lying in the cove eventually caused rot. The ill effects of the cove were most noticeable in the house where, of course, there

d

e

d) Barn with a bell-cast mansard roof and an unusual open cupola—perhaps a belfry. (Now demolished.) Location: l'Islet.

e) This is an old roof and so well built as to be proof against all weathers. The bell cast is not peculiar to Quebec, and may, like several in New Netherland in the United States, be of Flemish or Walloon origin. Only the gable is bell-cast. Location: St.-André.

a

b

c

d

e

f

a) The splendid Goulet barn demonstrates in its façade all the "departments" in the connected barn from threshing-floor doors to cattle at the far end. It has one of the finest mansard roofs in the province, and measures 125' x 25'.
Location: Lac St. Augustin.

b) Another example of the recessed wall and doors protected against the weather.
Location: Rue Notre Dame, Ancienne Lorette.

c) A whitewashed wall with a hole for the cat. Only in the tightly-sealed Quebec barn would a hole be necessary: in most barns, shrinkage in clapboard would provide a hundred exits for the mouser.
Location: same as *a*.

d) This stable wall might well be one in France at the time of Louis XIII. The posts and knee braces are each in one piece, except for trimming, just as they came from the tree.
Location: Bord d'l'eau. Portneuf County.

e) A very carefully designed façade. The area in deep shadow behind the segmental arch is a sheltered space with doors to byre and stable. The red door on the right marks the drive shed.
Location: St.-Pierre, Montmagny County.

f) An extension of the single, delightful sheltered area illustrated elsewhere on this page, reminiscent of the buggy sheds beside early village churches.
Location: west of St.-Gervais, Bellechasse County.

a

b

was a heat differential between the roof over a heated room and the roof over the unheated eave. In the barn, there was no such contrasting temperature unless one included the innocuous differential between the byre at animal heat of forty degrees and an outside of zero. Large sections of the barn would be zero or above, according to the insulation provided by snow and the covering of the roof.

In the seventeenth century the popular roof was thatch, even though the only materials available were straw or hay, both of which tended to get sodden, and both greatly inferior to the reeds of the homeland. In M. Bibeau's barn, the reader is looking at one of the last thatched barn roofs in Eastern Canada, and, while it is of comparatively recent date, its underside would be recognizable to a citizen farmer of the time of Louis XIV.

The fine Goulet farmstead reveals in elevation a feature characteristic of many French Canadian barns, the external expression of all its internal functions, and it is very simply done. Starting with the left, the drive floor is recognized by the wagon doors and two windows – only two, and quite small, because nothing inside at this point requires an excessive amount of daylight for either driving or storage. Further on, there is a secondary driving door followed by windows and normal domestic doors. This is the area of livestock, the windows admitting sufficient daylight for the health of cows and horses, and the doors balanced on the other side of the barn, adequate for their entrance or their escape.

The whole story of the animal end of the French Canadian barn is not yet told. A very practical element in the long Quebec barn is the ceiling over the livestock. It is used as extra storage for hay, but it will be quickly realized that it is also a blanket that adds greatly to the comfort of the animals below. In the Bibeau barn, it extends as far to the left as the partition separating the implements from the pigs. Over the same critical area in the Bherer barn, including the now-demolished sheep shed, the loft extends to include the first drive shed.

The itinerant thatcher no longer plies his trade in eastern Canada, but on the Canadian Prairies, one can still see houses and barns with mud walls, heavy thatched roofs,

and well trimmed eaves. The half dozen or so that remain in Quebec are tatty in appearance, and await only a decision for replacement on the part of the farmer. Will it be the well-tried cedar shingle, which in the old days succeeded thatch, or will it, in the absence of a pantile in most of North America, be one of those products of the new technology that one would regret? Even if cedar, it will be ⅜″ in thickness and not the hand-split shingles that were laid 1½″ thick in their butts at the eave and sometimes tapered in thickness toward the ridge. Many barns covered with slate have been recorded, perhaps the most notable being the one at New Lebanon, New York, but the matter of roof covering shows how lamentably badly off is the building industry in the east compared with Spain, Italy, California – even New Zealand and Australia, which have tile.

Surprising to people who do not know Quebec is the human, or should one say, animal scale of its old barns, which are in scale with the house whether that of seigneur or habitant, and with the landscape. There is, too, another element, a very human element, and that is the French Canadian love of pattern and colour which they succeed in expressing chiefly on their barn doors. This is a trait that the French Canadian shares with his neighbours in Pennsylvania, as the chapter on the barns of that state will show.

To close this section, acknowledgement must be accorded M. R. L. Séguin for so much that has been learned from his *Les Granges du Quebec*.[6] How thorough his research has been may be gathered from his lists of farmers and barn builders. In other places he takes us back to a far distant past, a past to be thought of in names like Louis XIII or XIV – of royal palaces and courtiers and not of barns and carpenters. One example will suffice: *"Bedard, Isaac-Baptisé vers 1616, à Saint-Sulpice de Paris. Épousa Marie Girard en 1645. Inhumé a Charlesbourg le 15 janvier 1689"* – a master carpenter, once the subject of Louis XIII.

a) A nice fanciful European touch to the gable peak.

b) Austere by comparison is this example of the roofer's craft in cedar shingles on a steep French gable. The pitch would suggest an earlier roof of thatch.

c

d

c) The atmosphere here is not of Quebec in the twentieth century, but of the seventeenth, and the thatched barn on the right adds to the illusion. The hay loft is above the drive shed and reached by a ladder. The photograph was taken in 1929.

d) A woodshed with roof projecting to form a porch. Location: les Eboulements, Charlevoix County.

e) Of all the systems of construction shown in these pages none is as unimpressive to the eye or as unusual as this one. It is not often found in English speaking North America, but is a technique of framing known as half lapping, with origins in Central Europe. The braces attached to the king post are pegged, but a close examination of the lowest junction will show that the post is so cut that the brace and post form a flush surface. See also 136b.
Location: St.-Urbain.

e

a

c

b

d

a) This little (20′ x 20′) sheep barn is in Quebec, but its prototype must surely be somewhere in the Swiss Alps. On the same principle as the Pennsylvanian forebay, the upper logs are cantilivered 3′9″ to give protection to the sheep below when they venture out in inclement weather.
Location: St.-Urbain.

b) Two methods of holding thatch in place can still be seen in Quebec. One, as we see in the illustration, is where logs are laid on the thatch at the ridge and crossed. (See also the Behrer barn [123d], where the logs were clearly visible in 1900.) The second eschews logs in preference to a ridge pole round which the thatch is lashed with thongs. Below the ridge, the technique is the same for both: the thatch is bound to birch rods or saplings running parallel to the eaves and resting on the rafters. Soon the thatched barns of Quebec will be a thing of the past. Already, the thatcher no longer plies his craft, and it is a matter of record that the crossed-log method was followed in Charlevoix County and the lashing to the ridge in Yamaska and St. Maurice Counties.
Location: north of St.-Hilarion, Charlevoix County.

c) The even line of the ridge of the roof indicates the second method of holding down the thatch.
Location: St.-Francois-du-Lac, Yamaska County.

d) The crossed poles at the ridge are clearly seen—a technique used in Charlevoix County. This is the reverse side of the barn in a.

e

f

g

e) This well-preserved thatched roof was done sixteen years ago. The uninterrupted ridge states clearly that the thatch was lashed to a ridge pole; hence nothing visible externally. A very lovely barn in keeping with its fine roof and over a hundred years old.
Location: St.-Francois-du-Lac.

f) A turkey house sheltered by the trees and built prior to such modern technological discoveries as chicken wire.
Location: St.-Urbain.

g) In this lovely old building, we see the simplest form of Quebec barn, the *habitant*. Its thatched roof clings precariously to life and the ridge pole round which the thatch was bound is exposed.

a

a) Frequently the exterior of a barn gives no indication of the spaciousness and scale of the interior. It is so with this venerable Bibeau barn. In this view taken from the loft over the byre, we see space after space identified by the "bents" or framework that divides them. Interesting too are the number of framing members still recognizable as trees shorn of their branches. Horse-drawn vehicles take a well-earned rest on what were once threshing floors.
Location: St.-Francois-du-Lac.

134

b

c

b) The undistinguished exterior conceals a great interior. This is a long, low Quebec barn with dimensions 100′ x 25′ and only 10′ to the eave.
Location: same as *a*.

c) A trough in a corner of the byre, carved out of the trunk of a tree. The halter or yoke on the left is an artifact not often seen so far as we know outside of Quebec.
Location: same as *a*.

a

b

c

a) The Bibeau interior: a museum piece much in its original condition. Here we see the birch rafter still with its bark, the cross saplings and the birch-bark thongs that laced everything together. Unfortunately, the straw was unworthy of the system that held it in place. Had it been the reeds that the immigrants knew in their homeland, how superb a roof outside this would have been from all points of view.
Location: same as 134*a*.

b) This is another example of half lapping. Where the diagonal brace meets the tie beam, this unusual framing technique is fully disclosed. The tie beam is cut on the diagonal to meet the full depth of the brace. The two are then flush and the peg locks them firmly together.
Location: same as 134*a*.

c) The barkless sticks in the illustration are redundant insofar as they affect the binding of the thatch to the saplings and the rafters. They are there to hold the farmer's tobacco crop and nothing else.
Location: same as 134*a*.

d

e

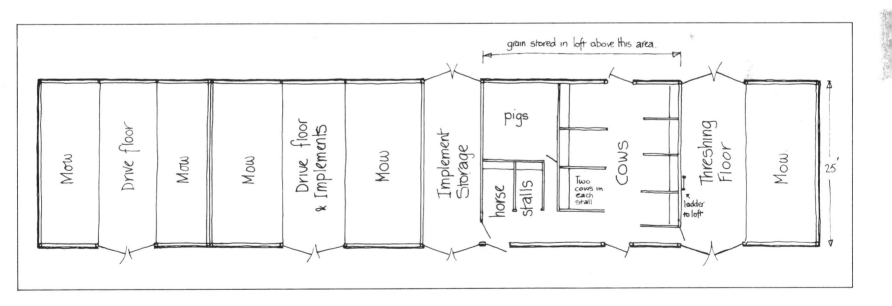

grain stored in loft above this area.

| Mow | Drive floor | Mow | Mow | Drive floor & Implements | Mow | Implement Storage | horse stalls | pigs | Two cows in each stall | Cows | ladder to loft | Threshing Floor | Mow |

25'

d) The reader may remember that in the English barn and others, bays were marked by single posts with continuous (though sometimes jointed) sills at the feet and plates at the head. In Quebec, we find a different construction, in which each bay is, as it were, a package with two posts and short separate plates and girts in each bay. Also to be noted is the diagonal corner bracing from tie beam to plate.
Location: St.-Francois-du-Lac.

e) This all-wooden "harr-hung" door is a very early method of swinging it without iron hinges.

a

b

d

a) A very interesting barn with recessed areas of different depths for different purposes. Quite dramatic is the ramp which rises from street level to the threshing floor behind the dormer. That, on the way, it plays havoc with the elliptical arch does not seem very important in the total picture.
Location: between Notre-Dame-du-Portage & St.-André.

b) This is another example of the recessed byre wall, with all the advantages of shelter for man on his chores and beasts basking in the sun in suitable winter

c

f

e

g

weather. The house is not attached and, while it may once have been a dwelling, it is now a milk house.

c) A barn chiefly notable for its fenestration, the unusual amount of glass, and its hipped roof.
Location: St.-Augustin (Portneuf).

d) A form of construction to be seen both in Quebec and in Europe. Instead of the common practice in which the rafter feet get their bearing from the plate, the rafters here oversail it and get stability from

sprockets, the short horizontal cut into the plate, and the vertical pegged into the rafters. Such a framing device does two things, it makes for a wide eave and clears the mow from queen, king, or other trusses.

e) Each gabled structure is a barn "fore and aft" and is connected by a low-roofed drive floor. A fall in the ground on the opposite side of the picture provides accommodation for livestock—the whole length of the rear. The barn measures 152' x 66'.
Location: Nicolet.

f) The feeling of unity that one gets in a view of this barn doubtless comes from the powerful horizontal line of the roof, but also from the builder's obvious pleasure in the ellipse on different openings and levels.
Location: Côte de Beaupré.

g) A barn with such unusual features as the hipped gable of the main roof and dormers, and fenestration on two levels. It is now demolished.
Location: L'Ange-Gardien.

a

b

c

a) This very compact little stable barn is chiefly remarkable for its great roof and its grand sweep to the eaves. Everything about it suggests that life within is snug and proof against the weather in any of its moods. Hay was stored in the roof and the walls are tight fitting plank and whitewashed in the Quebec custom.
Location: St.-Augustin.

b) This barn is well known for the sweep of its hipped roof, its wide projecting eave, and finely detailed cupola.
Location: St.-Augustin.

c) This is a picturesque scene of considerable interest for the variety of structural methods that it displays. To the right of the threshing-floor opening we see vertical planks, dressed logs (pièce sur pièce) and a frieze of boards beneath the eave. The passerby with romantic tastes, the architectural historian, and the artist would all get pleasure out of this barn.
Location: near Baie-St.-Paul.

Not all connected barns were irregular in their plan
arrangement and sky line, but the advantages of the
connection in regions where snow and cold were
endemic are clear. Firstly, the grouping about a courtyard gave protection from the wind, and, secondly, the
farmer could make the tour of his buildings under
cover from the warm kitchen of his house on the right.
Location: unknown, presumably Ontario.

Other Connected Barns

Although the New England and the Quebec barns are both connected and for the same reason, they are physically so dissimilar as to make it necessary to look at them separately. The former takes several forms, and its roof pattern is frequently irregular, while the latter, as we have seen, is compact like a trailer, its roof ridge uninterrupted, and its territory restricted to the province of Quebec.

The New England barn is found in several eastern states, and, quite properly, takes its name from the region where it is most common. At the same time, it is not unknown in Ontario, southern Quebec, Nova Scotia, and New Brunswick. If thought of only as an idea, quite divorced from architecture, it had much merit in those areas of North America where heavy snowfall was endemic rather than rare. Its unique feature, as will be remembered, was the house as an integral part of the farmstead. Happily, many are extant in that original form,[7] but in many more cases, the door in the wall that was common to house and barn has been closed, even bricked up, and the farmer is obliged to brave the storm before taking shelter in the nearest connected building. In the permanent closing of that quite ordinary door, a European tradition going back some two thousand years was broken.

In other instances, the farmer, emulating his neighbour with a separate dwelling, could perform a surgical operation on the house and remove it bodily from the barn to which it was attached, setting it up in its own garden some distance away. If we may consider such a decapitated barn as belonging to a category, we can include the many fine barns conceived as connected elements but without a house.

For such hygienic considerations as house flies and just plain smells, many settlers in New England and Canada eschewed one of the two basic advantages of the connected barn – the directness of access from kitchen to barn. More often, the woodshed or the carriage house provided a buffer between the two without interfering with the second advantage, the farmer's right of passage from home to barn under cover.

In its original form, it was a cozy arrangement for man and beast; the farmer made his visits to the barn in comfort, and, however violent raged the storm, the cattle would always be fed. Hovering over everything, however, was the ever-present menace of fire, which in the connected barn could be devastating and complete. So great was the danger that it is surprising that, as a type, it persisted as it has through the centuries. The town fathers in Lilly Eaton were aware of it in 1639, and a by-law passed in that year stated: "There being manni sad ascidantes in the Contree by fire, to the great damming of manny, by joining of barnes and haystackes to dwelling houses, therefor no barne nor haystacke shall be set within six polles of anni dwelling house opon panillte of twentie shillings."[8] This by-law is interesting not only for its wisdom and the obvious concern of the town councillors for the well being of the people in the community, but because of its date. There were, of course, other reasons than fire for the disappearance of the seventeenth- and eighteenth-century connected barns in New England, but fire must have accounted for many.

Looked at from the point of view of aesthetics, the New England barn defies analysis in conventional terms. It is not a building or complex of buildings that can be examined in the round for mass, proportion, fenestration, or the rhythm of repetitive parts. There are exceptions, but, in general, it is a whole series of elements running from the minimum cluster of house, woodshed, and barn in line or in an ell, to a string of many buildings forming no simple pattern. In such a large operation, the connected barn is much like a row of houses and shapes of pleasing design in the local vernacular on a village street. They conform to no set building line, but approach an imaginary sidewalk or retreat from it according to the fancy of a dozen owners who have but two things in common architecturally, the use of

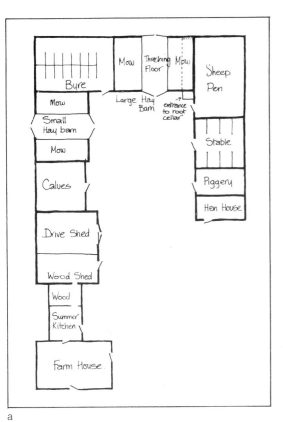

a

b

wood and the gable.

There are some connected barns for which this casual assemblage of elements would not apply. A unique example is the Warren Maxwell house at Weathersfield in Vermont.[9] The house itself must be one of the best known in the state both for its external appearance and the wealth of finely detailed woodwork within, but it stands out among connected barns because the conjunction consists of seven elliptical arches framing a passage between house and barn. Opening off this corridor and contiguous to the house are the kitchen and pantries, which take up three bays; the wagon shed takes up the next four, and then, the barn.

Such an ambitious architectural link would be striking in any connected barn, but this one is remarkable for being two storeys in height, and still low in its relationship to the house. The loft so formed is lit dimly by five small square windows, and was used as a cocoonery in the days when raising silk worms was, briefly, a Vermont industry.

It has already been noted that connected barns are almost invariably built of clapboard, with a minority in eastern New

England in shingle siding. In the twenty-six-hundred-mile survey he made, Dr. Zelinsky found only one connected barn in brick and none in log. Ontario was not part of his itinerary, but had it been, he would, probably, have enjoyed seeing the log connected barn of Mr. William Kidd near Ashton, Ontario. Mr. Kidd's is one of several magnificent log barns located, generally, in the neighbourhood of Ottawa. Unfortunately, the plan is indefensible in terms of travel and convenience. It is in an area notorious for the rigours of its winter, (recently achieving a record snowfall of one hundred and fifty inches); nonetheless, Mr. Kidd was obliged to leave the warmth and comfort of his kitchen to reach the barn.

In pursuit of the barn as architecture, areas have been explored where, because of geological or other factors, one kind of material would be found to dominate. The stone barn is rarely found singly. Clay country will likely be famous for its old brick houses, but less famous, unfortunately, for its brick barns, which in numbers must rank in North America well below wood and stone. When our oldest barns were built and the forests were bountiful, the farmer had his choice of clapboard, plank siding, or log, which the saw mills of the day were happy to provide. There are districts where one or the other predominates, but none is left with more reluctance than where the painted frame house sits in the shadow of a great log barn.

Not a few take on the basic form of buildings that are associated with the renaissance of classical architecture, and frequently indicate in their grouping the skill of a master even though they were created by a farmer manifestly untutored in the ways of Wren or Jefferson. Knowing that, one cannot help but be struck by what has been achieved in the realm of aesthetics, but there are other areas where the impact is more directly on the senses. Here one has to confess to being a romantic affected by the sight of logs of noble dimensions bowed with age and a century or more of exposure to winds, the cold of winter, and the heat of summer. From the same logs, many still wrapped in their forest bark, comes that pungent odour of cedar which, blended with that of nearby stacked hay, remains forever in one's memory.

a,b) This is a barn connected in all its parts, but Mr. Kidd the farmer, does have to go outdoors in order to perform his chores in the byre.

c) Buildings attached to each other like a child's set of house blocks, except that there is an underlying plan based on the comfort of the farmer as he goes about his chores.
Location: West Danville, Vermont.

d) This is a more compact solution, with the house, as always, at the head of the procession. It is also a colourful example, as the buildings are painted a uniform yellow ochre

c

d

a

a) This is the great Shaker barn at Hancock,
Massachusetts. First built in 1824, it suffered various
vicissitudes until 1865, when a barn much as we know
it today was built on the old foundations. It attracted
much attention as a new and exotic shape, and by the
1880's its design was given wide circulation. Like all
great architecture, its interior is inseparable from the
exterior and is, if anything, even more dramatic.

Circular and Polygonal Barns

Chapter 5

Circular and polygonal barns are all of the second half of the nineteenth century or later, and their territory covers most of agricultural North America. It would be interesting to know something about their builders –why they so ignored tradition as to embark on a structure involving elaborate setting up, the inevitable presence of pie-shaped rooms and consequent inconvenience, and the elimination of the help of neighbours in the old fashioned "bee."

While documentary proof is lacking, there must have been farmers with a flair for mathematics who knew the round barn enclosed the least wall area, and could calculate the comparative floor areas of square and circle, subtracting the corners. From that they would argue that they had an economical space in the circle and the advantage of a clean and easy sweep on threshing floor and cattle stalls.

History provides no evidence of primitive circular or polygonal barns, but the circular plan in house building goes back in Britain to the Bronze Age people whose round houses were constructed of unsquared boulders. In comparatively recent times, polygonal houses were not uncommon, though not all were as distinguished in their design or their occupants as the hexagonal house in Washington, known as the Octagon and the present headquarters of the American Institute of Architects. It was built in the 1790's and lived in for a time by President Madison following the burning of the White House. That very able architect, President Jefferson, built himself an octagonal summer house in Bedford County, Virginia, in 1806, and so taken was he with its shape that he flanked the house with octagonal privies in the manner of gazebos on an eighteenth century gentleman's estate.[1]

If by the forties of the last century the octagon had not achieved popularity, it was not the fault of Orson Squire Fowler, a phrenologist practising in New York, who wrote *A Home For All, or the Gravel Wall and Octagon Mode of Building:* a book that followed his success with *Amativeness or Evils and Remedies of Excessive Sensuality,* which went through forty printings.[2] His second book, like the first, was an enormous success and its influence immense.

Mr. Fowler's crusade for the octagon with a promise for a healthy and better life may have had an influence on barn building, though it is more likely that the decision to use so exotic a form was based more on whimsy than any philosophical concept of the health-giving properties that might be found inherent in its shape.

This would seem to be confirmed, even if an extreme case, in an octagonal farm house near Toronto built as a bird cage for a Mr. Bird. It was achieved by a frilly ginger bread verandah around the first story, out of which rose an octagon in pink brick with circular windows on each face. The octagon was terminated by a coved roof, which gave the illusion of upholding two chimneys united by an arch–a handle for a bird cage for all the world to admire.

But our concern is with octagonal barns and not with farm houses, however charming, and, if the ordinary rectangular barn is considered a vanishing landmark in North America, those of unusual geometric shape must be fast approaching extinction. There were never many, and now there are few.[3] Unfortunately, an analogy cannot be claimed with those rare species of birds whose continued existence is secured by pro-

b

b) The quality of the masonry can be judged from this detail.

a

b

vision for their breeding in captivity. The first circular barn in North America is a well-cared-for museum piece, the Shaker barn at Hancock, Massachussetts. It is likely to be the last as well as the first of its line.

Circular barns are almost certainly outnumbered by the polygonal, largely because the structural setting-up for the latter was easier and all contemporary building materials were available. The same was true for the circular, except that clapboard could be used only in barns of generous dimensions, and narrow boards, showing 3″–4″ exposure

a) Less substantial than the Shaker barn, but sturdy enough to survive continued use and abuse, is the polygonal barn near Edmonton, Alberta. Plans are afoot for its restoration as a civic project and few buildings could have a greater claim. In looking at the exterior, we are to imagine doors and windows as competently designed as the interior, and it is possible that parts of the clerestory were once glazed and shed abundant light on the central space. Date: 1897.

b) Of great significance in illustrations of barns in this

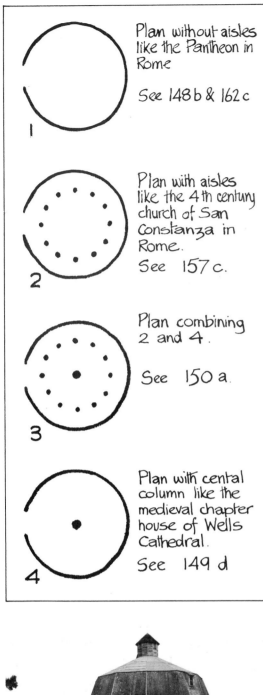

Plan without aisles like the Pantheon in Rome

See 148 b & 162 c

1

Plan with aisles like the 4th century church of San Constanza in Rome.

See 157 c.

2

Plan combining 2 and 4.

See 150 a.

3

Plan with central column like the medieval chapter house of Wells Cathedral.

See 149 d

4

d

c

to the weather, could be bent around the structural frame. Many beautiful barns were so built, but if set on the idea of the circular barn in wood, the farmer-designer could always use vertical planks or shingles with equally satisfactory results, or, alternatively, he could capture the feeling of the circle without the form by giving the barn ten or twelve straight sides. The visual effect, except at close quarters, is of a circular barn sheathed in the familiar horizontal boards.

Eric Sloane in his *An Age of Barns* has an interesting theory in regard to artifacts popular with the Shakers, Quakers and Holy Rollers, each of which shows a particular form with perfection as its aim. They were not alone in history in regarding the circle as the perfect form, and a predilection for it is shown in sewing circles, singing and prayer circles. "Farmers made circular designs on their barns, and their wives sewed circular patterns on quilts. The Shakers used the circle in their 'inspirational drawings'...they took delight in round hats, rugs and boxes; and they made round drawer-pulls and hand-rests for their severely angled furniture. There is a saying that the round barn was in-

tended 'to keep the devil from hiding in corners'."[1]

A farmer from Vermont or Quebec who was the owner of a circular or polygonal barn would find much that was familiar in many of the buildings of antiquity in Europe. He would, of course translate what he saw in marble columns and walls and floor of fine mosaic tiles to the barn at home, and, on a broader scale, he would recognize the circular central space, the surrounding aisle and the shafts of light from clerestory windows forming a pattern on walls and floor.

To see this, he might be standing in the fourth-century church of San Constanza in Rome, or in any one of several baptisteries that were built on the same basic principle of high central illuminated space and low aisles. The polygonal barn outside of Edmonton has all the characteristic features of the medieval baptistery, but has, in addition, a central post which forms the pivot and support for the radiating rafters. It is not too far-fetched to see in this structure another ecclesiastical proto-type—the chapter house at Wells Cathedral in which a central column merges with the ribbed vaulting of the ceiling.

chapter are the four plan types: (1) those without aisles; (2) those with nave and aisles; (3) the Edmonton example, with aisles and central post like a medieval chapter house; and (4) barns with or without aisle but with central silo. This circular barn is a perfect small sample of its type, with vertical boards and row of windows for the cattle in their stalls. Mr. Rempel, who took the photograph, is of the opinion that the mow is open space without a ring of posts forming an aisle.
Date: 1893 (approx).
Location: Hawkesbury, Ontario.

c) A very "architectural" small barn in which maximum storage of hay has been made possible by its dominating mansard roof. An all-glass cupola can be imagined, or it might have been a series of louvres for ventilation. Date: 1895 (approx).
Location: Thessalon, Ontario.

d) In this barn we see that clapboard can be applied to the circle in narrow boards. Its colour is red, complementary to the green grass, and a fitting background for the pattern of windows at different levels.

Outside diameter is 80 feet. Inside, the silo occupies the centre of the space which is aisle-less.
Location: three miles from Passumpsic, Vermont.

a

b

a) This is the interior of the Edmonton barn, and its dramatic structural effects are revealed. We are to picture it on two floors, the lower (below) showing the base of the central post in the cattle area, and the upper a combination of "baptistry" and "chapter house." The photographer has succeeded in getting a diffused illumination on everything, but how different had there been a clerestory which could flood the space with light from the sun. One cannot help but be fascinated by the thought that all the dignity and some of the grandeur of certain buildings of the Middle Ages have been captured here by a basic plan, the rhythm of bays formed by roughly trimmed tree trunks and the pattern of the rafters.
Location: southwest of Edmonton, Alberta.

b) This very daring piece of construction shows the base of the post below the mow, and the joists radiating from it that support the mow floor. And, of course, not only the floor, but the mow piled high with hay or straw. The concentration of forces on the post can be imagined.

c

d

e

In the Shaker barns at Hancock, a cluster of eight posts are required to support the lantern or cupola and the four windmill-like "trusses" that give extra stability to the structure. Not common are those polygonal barns in which a silo is the central feature–it may be contained within the roof, or surprisingly, emerge above it as in the stone Saskatchewan barn.

Like their ecclesiastical predecessors, the circular and polygonal barns had a plan arrangement based on use. The church was used for the assembly of people in the centre, and ceremonial processions in the aisle, while the barn established the major space for the storage of hay and the aisle for a variety of uses. Conceivably, a large circular barn could be built in which the aisle could be defined only by a parapet, but that would have produced a building with a diameter of say eighty feet[5] and a considerable number of problems to be solved in wood. The ring of posts reduced the diameter by as much as twenty-four feet at Hancock, which still left forty-eight feet in the mow. Consequently, only the smaller barns have a mow without aisles, and the uses to which the aisle was put

found accommodation elsewhere.

In few vernacular buildings do the dramatic effects of space and colour, of height and depth unfold as they do in the circular barn with aisle. No better example could be found than the Shaker barn at Hancock, and the visitor cannot help but be astonished as he enters the great doorway, and stands at a railing overlooking the mow. He will involuntarily look down some ten feet or so, and in his mind's eye, because the barn is now no longer in use, see the extraordinary spectacle of the heads of cattle facing into the mow from which they were fed. Thirty feet above him he will see a superb ceiling in which rafters radiate from the ring of the cupola, and light from cupola and clerestory combine to cast a glow on piled hay in daytime and almost a flame at sunset.

This was, and still is, an astonishing architectural monument to the skill of its designer, and the masons and carpenters who put it together in 1865 on the foundations of an earlier one of 1824. Not surprisingly, it attracted much attention as a new and exotic shape in Massachussets, and over the years drew increasing numbers of the proponents

c) The exterior in miniature.

d) The post and the radiating rafters of the clerestory roof.

e) The clerestory is boarded up, but what light shows in one bay gives an indication of the effect that may once have been obtained by areas of glass.
It will be noted that the post also served as a ladder.

a

b

d

c

a) The alley from which the cattle were fed. Hay would be forked from the mow on the right to the floor, and thence to the cattle with heads in the stanchions on the left.
Location: Shaker Village, Hancock, Massachusetts.

b) The cows are to be imagined in their stalls with heads looking into the mow. In particular, this view shows the massive timbers used as posts and joists for the support of the threshing and drive floors.

c) The number and size of the windows on the Shaker barn are unusual.

d) Not a little of the drama in the Shaker barn comes from the scale of the interior, and the octagon of posts supporting the cupola and forming a base from which the rafters radiate. Impressive, too, are the four great windmill-like braces (each 23'10'') which span the mow from octagon to posts on the drive floor. If one is fortunate enough to spend a day here, he will witness the unforgettable sight of the cold morning light, the warmth of noon, and the red glow of evening on golden brown timbers.

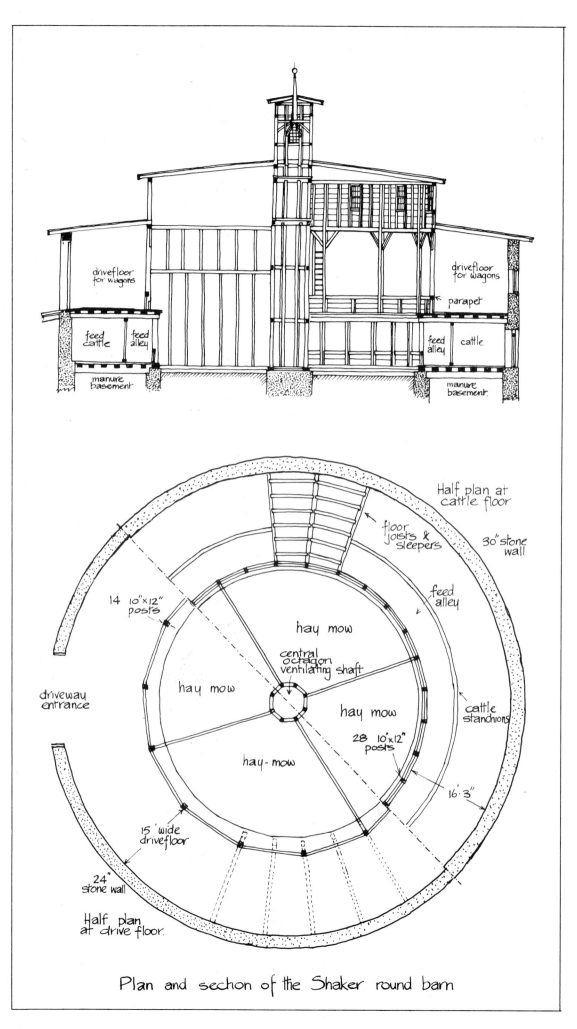

driverfloor for wagons

drivefloor for wagons

parapet

feed cattle

feed alley

feed alley

cattle

manure basement

manure basement

Half plan at cattle floor

floor joists & sleepers

30" stone wall

14 10"x12" posts

feed alley

hay mow

central octagon ventilating shaft

hay mow

hay mow

cattle stanchions

driveway entrance

28 10'x12" posts

hay-mow

16' 3"

15' wide drivefloor

24" stone wall

Half plan at drive floor.

Plan and section of the Shaker round barn

a) Not only do the rafters radiate, but so do the floorboards. Given the patience and the skill of the Shaker carpenter brethren, nothing else would be so pleasing.

b) A view showing the cattle stalls illuminated, the windmill-like braces which divide the mow in four, and the parapet to the drive floor from which everything can be seen—horizontally and vertically.

154

a

b

and publicists of the new "scientific agriculture." By the 1880's, its design was given wide circulation in the leading farm journals.

"As progressive farmers on the Great Plains were advised, so they built, and during the last two decades of the century timber variants of the Round Stone Barn appeared nearly everywhere along the western frontier. A number still survive, especially in Kansas, Nebraska, and the Dakotas, providing to this day the tribute of imitation to what an agricultural writer of the mid-century called 'the superb ingenuity of the Shaker builders of Hancock, whose circular barn should always stand as a model for the soundest dairying practices'."[6]

In *Dairy Farming,* a book published in the United States in 1879, a chapter was devoted to the merits of the "American Octagonal Barn" over the rectangular, in the expectation that it would prove a boon to the dairy farmer. The two principal advantages of the eight-sided barn, as the writer saw it, were economy of material, and the open floor, uncluttered by posts, for the free handling and storage of hay. As an example of economy, he cites an octagonal barn designed to replace four standard barns destroyed by fire. The old barns had a "basement area of 7,000 square feet and the octagon only 5,350 – yet the internal capacity of the latter was greater." The writer saw no structural difficulty in designing an octagonal barn for a thousand-acre farm without aisle posts 150 feet in diameter. He gives a specification describing the timbers that would go into his great barn, and sums up by saying "its external form being that of an octagon cone, each side bears equally upon every other side, and has great strength without cross ties or beams. It requires no more material or labour than the ordinary roof."

The editor comments in conclusion that the octagon will not likely recommend itself to English notions because it is so totally different from anything to which his countrymen were accustomed. Even in North America, the octagonal barn with a clear span of 150 feet in wood would have caused a sensation in 1879 as it would in 1972.

Later in these pages, the reader will see a remarkable barn at St. Benoît, Quebec, that is over seventy feet in diameter, remarkable as architecture, but even more because it was

c) An old stone prairie barn, with its unmistakable silo. Remembering the troubles that Mother Francoise Juchereau had with masonry in Quebec in the seventeenth century (see "The Connected Barn"), one wonders how the cattle fared here in a prairie winter. Location: near Regina, Saskatchewan.

c

155

a

b

designed empirically without benefit of the structural engineer with his precise knowledge of how timber of given dimensions behaves under tension or compression in normal or adverse conditions. It took a brave man to build the barn at St. Benoît.

In the illustrations that follow, it will be seen that all the dramatic architectural qualities to be found in the circular barn will be discovered also in the polygonal and, as has been said before, the more sides to the barn, the greater the difficulty, visually, in distinguishing one from the other.

Summary
Site:
The site for circular and polygonal barns is, ideally, flat, with a broad ramp leading to the wagon doors, but not infrequently such barns are banked.

Use:
In nearly all samples seen, the barn served the customary uses of the traditional rectangular barn, i.e. the ground floor was fully occupied by livestock, and the second by the storage of fodder and implements.

Plan:
Plan takes two forms – the mow with aisle in the larger barns, and the aisleless space in the smaller. The usual arrangement of stalls, except that they are radial, is found on the ground floor.

Section:
There is considerable variation in section through such barns. Unique, probably, is the Shaker barn, where the section shows the floor of the cattle stalls as an extension of the floor of the mow. Hence, as described in the text, the spectacle of a row of cattle heads looking into the mow from which they were fed. More often, the mow floor and the cattle floor are separate, one above the other as in a rectangular barn.

Materials:
All traditional materials are found in the construction of the polygonal barn – wood in the form of clapboard, plank (vertical), cedar shingles, "stovewood," stone, and brick. The curvature of the circular barn will determine the suitability of clapboard – if sufficient, it can be bent to the curve.

a) The long enclosed ramp to the barn. Like other elements in this famous barn, the detailing of dormers and ventilators is of a high order.
Location: near St.-Benoît-du-Lac, Quebec.

b) The interesting massing of barn, ramp, silo, ventilating "chimneys," and cupola of the same great barn.

c

c) There is neither silo nor central post to St.-Benoît.
The uncluttered floor is made possible by a "superb
roof of radiating rafters."

157

a

c

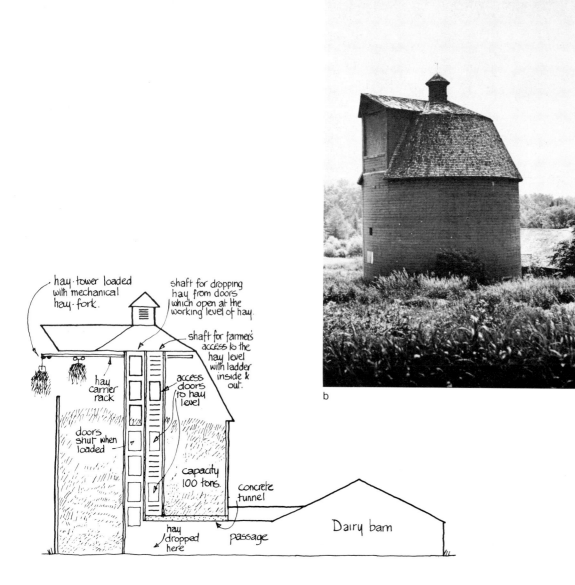

b

hay·tower loaded with mechanical hay·fork.

shaft for dropping hay from doors which open at the working level of hay.

shaft for farmers access to the hay level with ladder inside & out.

hay carrier rack

access doors to hay level

doors shut when loaded

capacity 100 tons.

concrete tunnel

Dairy barn

hay dropped here

passage

a) The roof of the hay tower at the farmstead near St.-Benoît-du-Lac invites comparison with the best of the vernacular architecture of any country. To describe it as breathtaking is not an exaggeration.

b) Hay was lifted by pulley arrangement to the open door in the dormer. No one would guess that this small ochre-coloured building housed so magnificent a roof.

c) This striking view has to be studied along with the sketch section. One learns that at peak load the farmer

would climb the steps in the tower and drop hay down
a shaft to the basement, from which it was taken by
tunnel to the cattle in the byre. This ingenious device
was born of the need to do everything possible under
cover in winters of deep snow. As the hay pile
decreased with use, the farmer could operate through
doors in the tower according to the level of the hay.

a

b

a) Forgetting the lean-to on the left, one is immediately
impressed by the symmetry of this barn, both in its com-
position and the unusual concentration of windows
above the central door. The severity of the sides and
absolute austerity of the end elevation would indicate
the need for enclosure above all else. Surprisingly, the
exterior shows no evidence of ventilation in any form,
except for the two closed hay doors.
Location: L'Enfant Jésus, Quebec.

b) Side elevation of the barn in a.

c

d

e

c.d) Unusual indeed is this circular clapboarded barn—obviously an object of joy to its owner, or he would not have gone to the trouble of crowning the façade with a battlemented parapet, and a matter of pride for the neighbours who have named the road after it.
Location: near Glen, New York State.

e) Since the photograph was taken, the roof has been completely altered. The lower storey is part masonry, part stovewood.
Location: Lafontaine, Ontario.

a

b

c

a) Known locally as the Pepper Pot, this octagonal barn is a landmark in the locality. The illustration shows a beautiful roof, and light from the clerestory shines on the ingenious arrangement of timbers that are part of the mow.
Location: Erin, Ontario.

b) The illustration of this octagonal barn hardly needs explanation. The cattle floor is well defined by windows, and the earth ramp leads boldly up to the bright red wagon doors at the threshing floor level. The St. Lawrence River can be seen in the distance.
Location: St.-Roch-des-Aulnaies, Quebec.

c) Another complicated system of braces fanning out to the rafters in the barn alongside. A clear span is thus provided below free from posts.

d

e

d) This barn was first seen in deep snow which was crimson from reflection of the painted shingle walls. It piles up beautifully to a roof in two slopes terminating in the cupola and well-designed flue stack. Inside are nave and aisles, and a strong, many-sided central silo. Location: near West Brome, Quebec.

e) The central silo of the West Brome barn.

a

a) This fine barn has an almost Russian skyline when first seen at sunset. It requires study, as while it appears a square and is one, it is nevertheless an octagonal barn squared at the corners. The smooth valleys in the shingled roof show how the parts are joined. The porch-like structure is a milk house. Whitewash in Quebec follows a tradition going back to the Middle Ages in Britain and Europe. Westminster Hall was whitewashed for Edward I (1239–1307). Location: near St.-Anselme, Quebec.

b) A less striking barn, with a curious ceiling, is this one. Its interior is marked by a single-span roof without supporting posts. The unusual rounding-off of the roof below the cupola accounts for the structure seen in the next illustration.
Location: St.-Anselme, Quebec.

c) The rafter patterns of the barn in b resemble a gigantic crab. Its intricacy and beauty can best be seen against the light within the cupola. It is not too far-fetched to compare some of these late nineteenth-century structures with the intricate stone vaulting of the medieval church. In both cases, the ceiling design was conceived without professional architectural or engineering aids.

b

c

d

d) An Ontario barn interior remarkable for the hay-lifting device which revolves about the central post. Location: near Fullerton, Ontario.

a

a) A striking twelve-sided barn with central silo and (barely discernible on the right) a long, completely covered ramp. The framing of the roof gives a dome-like effect to the exterior.
Location: near Waitsfield, Vermont.

b) A peaceful scene in which the many-sided barn acts as a background to the charming little building that has served at various times as milk house and spring house, and is now a granary. How snugly it fits into the broad ramp leading to the red wagon doors.

b

166

c

d

e

Location: Highway 23, near Ste.-Marie, Quebec.

c) The cap of the cupola that landed in the woods. Location: see *e*.

d) A most colourful barn, and so characteristically French. The dark roof contrasts with the whitewashed walls and the bright red wagon doors get added importance at the head of the ramp. Elsewhere in these pages we shall note the prevalence, not only in Quebec, of the square windows that define the byre and stable.
Location: Ste.-Marie, Quebec.

e) What does one say about a barn like this, and what of its builder? It has been said elsewhere in this chapter that the designers of circular and polygonal barns showed extraordinary ingenuity in structural framing, and no less in the architectural massing of such elements in the fabric as the silo and cupola. We have referred among ourselves to this barn as "the theatre" because of its resemblance in silhouette to the Shakespeare Memorial theatre in Stratford, Ontario.
Location: Mystic, Quebec.

a

a) More of the barn at Mystic, in which we see its exciting interiors. For the first time in this book, we see how the industrial revolution affected the barn. The man who epitomized the structural and mechanical achievements of this age was the inventor, whose handiwork can be seen in the gears in the roof that once operated a turntable in the floor–and yet the exterior proclaims him a product of the Romantic Movement. The critic will observe how precisely and nicely the clerestory at the feet of the white roof spaces is detailed. Cast iron or steel rods used in the ceiling

show how technology had caught up with the farmer. The owner was both the designer and the manufacturer of farm implements.

b) It is sad to see so fine a barn in tatters. The clapboards are very narrow, but in exposed parts (beside post or right side) one can see heavy interior planks.

c) Each of the gables frankly exposed on the exterior marks the end of a space or room that is an extension of the mow. Some have been used for animals, but

generally they were for the storage of hay and could be closed off from the mow by doors, as shown in the illustration. Another look at the mechanical "heart" of the interior (the gears, etc., in the ceiling) he will see "rails" (obviously not rafters) going off to the right. These operated mechanical hay forks which dropped the hay into whichever of the several "mows" required it.

b

c

a

b

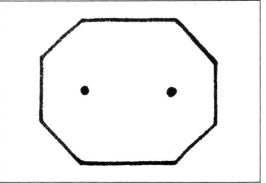

a) This barn ranks high for structural ingenuity among the polygonal barns of Quebec. The basic plan is an elongated or extended octagon to which lean-tos have been added
Location: near St.-Charles.

b) Understanding of the interior will be simplified by considering the extended octagon as a central rectangular space with an "apse" at each end. On the centre of the diameter of the apse is a post which supports the roof assisted by braces forming an

c

interesting fan pattern.

c) Looking at this hilltop barn on a cloudy day, the
spectator might well think of the Bastille and unspeak-
able suffering behind its prison-like windows. He would
be wholly wrong. It is one of the several fine circular
barns in Vermont. Its colour is a faded moss green
over narrow boards, its roof is orange, and, in every
way, the barn is a sheer delight to behold. Its size can
Location: near Lowell, Vermont.

Part 3

The Decorative Arts

A lintel from a barn in Erin Township, Ontario, now at
the Rockwood Academy.

When your barn is well fill'd all snug & secure

Be thankful to God & remember the poor

1863

173

a

a) Light streaming into the mow illuminates hay and
time-worn timbers.

Whenever the barn has appeared in these pages, it has been viewed for the interest of its architectural form as a three dimensional object in a varied landscape, and for an appreciation of its aesthetics in terms of structural framing and the forming of its internal spaces. In the architecture of our time, paramount importance is attached to the psychological effect of space on the spectator, and more particularly, of contrasting spaces at different levels. Obviously, this aesthetic experience is not possible of realization in every building type, but it is possible in the

barn, and to a high degree. It is achieved quite naturally and simply by the juxtaposition of different functional elements, quite often seen at different levels and in areas of different heights. It is to be seen and appreciated in the English barn as much as in the great Pennsylvania barn.

In the old barns which are the subject of this book, the interior of each may be admired for the majesty of its timbers, both horizontal and vertical, but more important is the vision of the interior exposed as a room, in which the eye is drawn from the comparative lowness of one area to the more spectacular height of the central space, illuminated or not by cupola or clerestory.

The sensation created by these contrasting elements has been exploited in architecture by persons in ages as different as the church and barn builders of the Middle Ages and Frank Lloyd Wright in our own era. Other things, too, contribute to the pleasurable sensation created by the barn interior – such things as the rhythm of bays formed by tall timbers, the colour of well-worn boards, and unconsciously, the awareness of the miracle of the framing held together by mortice and tenon and dowels of oak or hickory.

All of this, of course, is experienced in the lofty space of the mow, and it must be confessed that, compared with the worshipper in the cathedral whose view is obscured only by people like himself, the spectator in the barn may have his view, depending on the season, completely eclipsed by bales of hay piled into the high shadows of the roof, and implements, often obsolete, of monstrous proportions. However, with imagination, and a clue to the artistic treasures to be enjoyed, he will see beyond the hay and the reaper and binder to the beauty of the space surrounding him.

There can be few wholly functional buildings of past centuries that can create so satisfying an impression, few where the design is based solely on need, and few where the structure destined to meet that need is everywhere exposed. The barn interior represents functional, vernacular architecture at its best. It depends for its effect on the arrangement of spaces, on material and natural light, often casting beams from unexpected sources. It is entirely free from extraneous aids in paint or any other medium.

Primitive man adorned his cave with paintings of animals and scenes from the

b

b) The interior of each may be admired for the majesty of its timbers, both horizontal and vertical, but more important is the vision of the interior exposed as a room in which the eye is drawn from the comparative lowness of one area to the more spectacular height of the central space, sometimes illuminated by cupola or clerestory.
Location: near Ayton, Ontario.

a

b

hunt, and the same desire for colour, if more sophisticated, can be seen in the majority of North American homes. Less common in the new world is evidence of man's desire to enliven the exterior of his dwelling with paint, but there are people in Europe and Asia with a long tradition of polychromy in the treatment of their houses. Among them are the Swiss and the Germans, who paint not only their houses but also their barns in brilliant primary colours, with particular attention to beams, joist and rafter ends which are exposed in their national tradition of timber framing. The difference between the cheerful Swiss and German houses and their barns, and the urban or rural house of North America, is so striking as to suggest a joyful though disciplined use of colour on the one hand and a puritanical avoidance of it on the other.

For several reasons, the immigrant German and Swiss did not carry their tradition of colour in domestic architecture to the New World. For one thing, paint was limited to only a few colours, none of them to be compared with the blues, reds or yellows of the homeland. At the Shaker Village at Hancock, Mass., three colours were employed, each on a different building. Two were made from natural earths and the third, white, was expensive in the early nineteenth century and reserved for special buildings – in the case of the Shaker Village, for the chapel. The earth colours were a Dijon mustard tone of ochre and a reddish purple.

The limitation of these muted colours would be sufficient reason for the absence of a polychromatic scheme of decoration on the North American barn, but a second reason might have been the absence of those exposed structural members in say, the Swiss barn, that by their very nature seemed an invitation to the painter. From the time of the early Egyptians and the Greeks, these structural elements have been the effective basis for a colour scheme, and, while present in the North American barn, they were relatively unimportant. Rafter ends were rarely striking, and, only in the forebay of the banked barn are heavy joists exposed. They were often roughly shaped timbers retaining their bark and hardly a subject for polychromy.

Fortunately, colour is not entirely absent in the rural scene, and among the most colourful of vernacular buildings is the barn

– not in the sense of an organized scheme of decoration, but rather of an overall painting of the structure with areas picked out for special attention.

Red has been a favourite colour for barns in all countries, especially Scandinavia, and may have been selected intuitively by the farmer because it complements the surrounding green fields. White is a close runner-up to red in popularity, and apart from its obvious value as contrast to roof and ground, it may subtly suggest an immaculate operation within. The black and white barn might not seem appropriate to an urban expert who did not know the countryside, but in practice it has a suitability and a dignity quite secondary to the fact that the farmer's distinguished herd might be Holstein. But not all barns are painted; many, as will be seen, are brick or stone, and the weathered grey pine boarded barn has its own inimitable beauty, and calls for no artificial aids.

No one can travel through the countryside of Pennsylvania without being conscious of the colourful circular patterns on barn walls, commonly called hexes, without asking himself whether these hex signs were there originally to ward off evil spirits, or whether, as now, they were purely decorative, or in the local vernacular, "chust for nice."

It would seem unnecessary to define the word "hex," as it is part of the language of North America where to put a hex on anyone is readily understood, but not seriously feared. It finds no place in the Oxford English dictionary, but Random House says "to bewitch, spell or charm, usually associated with witchcraft—derivation German—*Hexe,* a witch".

There is no doubt that in their first forms, the six-pointed star, sometimes called the tulip pattern, and the whirling swastika were ancient folk-designs "predating the alphabet, and recognized as part of the cult of sun worship which ruled pre-Christian Europe for over 1,500 years. The six-pointed compass star is found on a Mycenaean gold disk made about 1550 B.C. and the revolving swastika on a Roman stone quarry by German labourers. These round and radiating symbols of a forgotten religion have been preserved by the clannish Germans from their ancient peasant culture. Originally representing the power of the sun over seasons, crops and life,

a) Swirling swastika carved on a hutch cupboard in Ontario.

b) The six-pointed star like the swastika is a symbol going back to remote times in European history—also on a hutch cupboard.

176

c

they are particularly appropriate to the Pennsylvania Dutchman who still consults the signs of the Zodiac at planting time."[1]

In the state of Pennsylvania, history and legend are lost in hex patterns of infinite but not always pleasing variety, sold by commercial interests to farmers merely as decorations. One cannot be too critical of the purchasers because the best conceived designs do little damage in terms of aesthetics, and no less a person than Louis XIV took a many-pointed star as the symbol of himself as Sun King for his own royal advertising purposes.

Historically, both the six-pointed star and the whirling swastika were widely used in Pennsylvania before they appeared on barns, and examples can be seen on tombstones, bibles, riding saddles, and the sometimes extensive decoration on mugs and dower chests, where one can be sure they were enjoyed for themselves and had no sinister connotations.

In an interesting article on butter moulds, Earl F. Robacker illustrates both star and swastika, and "guesses" that, from the evidence of the same patterns to be seen in marriage frakturs and dower chests, both go

c) The carpenter leaves his mark indicating that this particular framing is for the third "bent", or one of the prefabricated trusses that divide the barn longitudinally. The tenon of course is hidden, but the hardwood pegs show how it was so securely held.

177

a

b

a) Colour and light and the rhythm of bays separating the "nave" from the "aisle". The space is divided by eight great "bents" in a barn 165 feet long. Location: near Hyndford, Ontario.

b) The afternoon light illuminates the framing of the barn in which posts, girts, braces, and studs can be identified.

d

e

c

c) Location: near Clifford, Ontario.

d) The white barn is a close runner-up to red in popularity and, apart from its obvious value as contrast to roof and ground, it may subtly suggest an immaculate operation within.
Location: Highway 219, Somerset County, Pennsylvania.

e) Black and white are favourite colours for the barn, especially in lush grass country. The combination is an obvious one as a shelter for a herd of Holsteins, but more often is admired for itself.
Location: near Ballinafad, Ontario.

f) The opposite of black and white in startling contrast is seen in this barn, where a most harmonious relationship is achieved through yellow ochre-painted boards and faded cedar shingles.
Location: near Sloansville, New York.

f

back to the seventeen- and eighteen-hundreds.[2] One writer quotes "oldsters" as saying that these were the only patterns used prior to 1900, while another, also anonymous, finds the star closely resembling the central theme on silver amulets once worn by pregnant women in the Sudan. Inscribed in Arabic, these objects sought well-being for the wearer. Turkish soldiers, desert Arabs, and Indian Muslim women wore similar ornaments. Dr. Preston A. Barba extends the field still farther when he comments on the common use of the six-pointed star on the gravestones of Pennsylvania German settlers. He finds the same design in such widely separate places as on the temple steps of ancient Ephesus, on the walls of the Byzantine Metropole church of Athens, and on the bronze doors of the shrine of Eyoub Ensaai at Istanbul. He agrees that, along with the whirling swastika, they form the two basic designs on the barns of Pennsylvania.[3] In short, evidence is not lacking that in Europe and Asia the star and swastika were used from remote times as symbols with implications, usually, of goodwill.

The swastika is always shown as whirling, and its root is the Sanskrit word *svasti,* or "well being" (*su*–good, *asti*–being).[4] It is a surprise to find this ancient German symbol having an even more remote origin in India, and, far from casting a sinister shadow, bearing a message of friendliness and humanity.

The use of these symbols from the dawn of history until modern times is indisputable, but what is the evidence that they were brought here by the early European settlers of Pennsylvania and other states, and, if so, what was their significance? Patricia Mullen states unequivocally that the "hex or witch-foot" was brought over from the Rhineland by Mennonites and the Amish when they settled here (Pennsylvania) in the seventeenth century. Then they were used to ward off cow-fever, but, today, they are "chust for nice," and, in case, "for luck".[5]

A similar view was held by Dr. John Stoudt: "It has been demonstrated that the persecuted Mennonites and other sectarians of Europe, being in an inhospitable country, marked their barns and houses with these signs so that their fellow sectarians would know that hospitality could be found within.[6]

Finally, as it affects the barn, we have Mr.

Wallace Nutting writing nearly fifty years ago: "The ornaments on barns found in Pennsylvania go by the local name of hexafoos or witchfoot. They are supposed to be a continuance of a very ancient tradition, according to which these decorative marks were potent to protect the barns, or more particularly the cattle from the influence of witches. The hexafoos was added to its decoration as a kind of demoniac lightning rod." This statement was the first to draw attention to the hex, and to discern a message more important than mere decoration, but it was attacked by Dr. Alfred Shoemaker who described it as "balderdash, fiddlesticks and nonsense." The defence came from none other than the former chief of the Folklore Division of the State Historical and Museum Commission, Dr. Henry Shoemaker: "hex signs are not for decoration...their connection with superstition regarding witchcraft, spells and hexing cannot be doubted."[7]

History, inherited beliefs, and customs are no longer with us when we come to the attractive white line around doorways and windows on the barns of more than one state. At first sight, they suggest elegance and charm, especially on a red or black barn, and one is surprised to read of a once fairly widespread belief that they were intimately connected with witchcraft, indeed with the devil himself. One Pennsylvania folklore publication has this to say of it: "To keep the devil out of your barn, paint a white line around your barn door much higher than the door itself. When the devil opens the door, he will not stop and will run against the line. He will not return."[8] One can only say that such a trust does a grave injustice to the intelligence of both the farmer who painted the lines and to the devil himself.

Examples abound of quite interesting, often spectacular decorative star patterns in wood which resemble in technique the large fret-saw board designs on "ginger bread" houses. They tell no story, but obviously satisfy some urge for expression in beauty on the part of the farmer or his wife. They are almost always geometric in design, the exception, and perhaps the only one of its kind, being the crossed-American-flag motif on the barn of Mr. R. W. Zweizig's farm near Hamburg, Penn. The barn is known as the Zehner barn, and recalls the first Amish bishop in America, who is buried nearby.

a) The Christ on a barn in Quebec.
Location: Ile d'Orléans.

a

b

c

Before the appearance of the mammoth billboards that today advertise everything from soft drinks to bank loans and add to the visual pollution of the countryside, there were "messages" on the barns. Some are merely factual and give the farmer's name along with the name of his herd, some are naive; few will meet the highest typographical standards, but all are large, and, if fresh, legible. In Canada, farmers are met who remember a time when an enterprising salesman would agree to paint the barn in exchange for permission to flaunt the name of his product in a prominent place. Startling effects were obtained by white letters saying "Castoria" on a red barn, or red on a black and white barn, with the exhortation to "Chew Bull Durham" or the implied delights of Mail Pouch Tobacco and Old Chum.

More common, and without consideration for the smoker and the constipated except to turn their thoughts to higher things, are the religious texts on the barns on the highways and by-ways of the land. Even the loneliest barn on the least used country lane will have a sign exhorting the passerby to "Get right with God," or, in more settled communities, "Thou shalt not covet thy neighbour's wife Ex. 20.27." By and large, such signs are, of course, most often found in the religious settlements of Mennonite or Amish folk, but not always. The urge to display a message by pious people is not restricted to barns or any particular sect, as texts on granite boulders and cliffs in state or national parks testify only too clearly.

Fine lettering in stone is rare, if only because most North American barns are in wood. Not infrequently on the heavy timbers inside the barn, the farmer has carved his initials and the master carpenter his identifying symbols at the critical meeting place of structural members. Poor incised lettering is rarely seen. The discovery of a decorated stone lintel from the door head of an old barn was a major find at Rockwood, near Guelph in Ontario. Four pointed stars in circles flank beautifully incised letters with the words "When your barn is well filled all snug and secure, Be thankful to God & remember the poor." Over all is the date 1863. The dimensions of the stone are impressive: its length is 11'4", height 1'2", and thickness 1'0".[9]

Less spectacular, but fine, is the sheaf of wheat carved on the keystones of segmental

b) Monumental indigenous architecture—the great granaries of Galicia. The curious mushroom-shaped supporting columns are flaired to make climbing difficult for the rats.

c) Before the appearance of the mammoth billboards that today advertise everything from soft drinks to bank loans, and add to the visual pollution of the country-side, there were messages on the barns—the one illustrated is extremely restrained.

b

a) Hexes of traditional design about the turn of the century. To quote one authority: ''The hexafoos are supposed to be a continuance of a very ancient tradition according to which these decorative marks were potent to protect the barns, or, more particularly, the cattle, from witches.'' They are preserved today only for their decorative value, or, in the local vernacular, ''chust for nice.''

b) A barn famous in Pennsylvania for the number and brilliance of its decorations.
Location: New Smithville, Pennsylvania.

a

a

b

arches on a stone barn not far distant from the lintel. Sculpture of any kind on a barn represents loving care and a desire on the part of the farmer and his mason to do something of permanent beauty, and it is unfortunate that it is so rare.

Where sculpture was not to be had for reasons of cost or lack of a sculptor in the community, the farmer could express his feeling for beauty by a weather vane, or more simply, strap hinges on a barn door. The weather vane may sit squarely on the barn ridge, or, better, on the coved roof of a cupola. It may take the simplest of all shapes, the arrow, or, while very rare, a fish in silhouette. Most popular is the horse, and most appropriate is the rooster. One can imagine that not a day would pass when the farmer who once was the proud possessor of either of our cockerels, would not look up for sign of a wind. Was it a "winnowing" wind blowing across the threshing floor, or was it east, bringing rain to alter the schedule for the day. Whether fish or fowl, it could be counted on to raise the farmer's spirit in the cold light of dawn.

No part of North America, unless it be Pennsylvania, offers so much in colour decoration in its vernacular architecture as the province of Quebec. Particularly is this true of its barns. Wayside shrines are still to be seen in the countryside, though many show signs of neglect, but to find a statue of the Christ over a barn door, a white and gold figure in a niche, is more arresting because of its humble surroundings than if it were on the façade of a medieval cathedral. The cross is not found on Quebec barns, but is a familiar symbol on the granaries of Galicia in Spain and of other Catholic countries in Europe.

The Québecois love colour, and it finds expression on the barn in the painting of the wagon doors in brilliant colours in an infinite variety of designs. In many cases, they are so competent as to suggest a close association between the farmer and the École des Beaux Arts or the École des Meubles in Montreal, but it is not so: they are the spontaneous creations of the habitant farmer.

Along with its hex patterns, Pennsylvania more than any other state or province revels in its paintings of cattle and horses. Always in silhouette, because that presented no great problem in draftsmanship for the amateur

a) Sculpture of any kind on a barn represents loving care and a desire on the part of the farmer to do something of permanent beauty. It is unfortunate that it is so rare. This sheaf-of-wheat keystone comes from a barn near Elora, Ontario. See also 98*a*.

b) Barn sculpture of the highest order. The date 1866 was carved in a shield below the keystone. Location: same as *a*.

artist, they are nevertheless arresting and, in the most effective way, announce the breed or the animal for which the farm is known.

Most unusual is a painting of horses heading into the picture in motion and foreshortened. This represented an unusual skill, and one not likely to be attempted by the farmer or his wife who painted in water colours. It was found on a door in New Brunswick and still in fair condition. Popular once were the Clydesdale and Percheron draught horses, noble beasts, now rarely seen as mural decoration on gable or wagon doors. These were the horses bred in late medieval times to carry a knight into battle, and so great was the weight of armour plus, let us say, a rider of the weight of Henry VIII, that only a charger of Clydesdale or Percheron dimensions had the strength not only to support the load, but attack an enemy who was similarly mounted. Such splendid beasts once served their purpose on the farm, but today are bred chiefly for show. Those who remember the parade of brewers' or coal merchants' horses will recall their glistening coats, the powerful chests and hindquarters, their curled manes and tails, the noise of bells, and the clumping of hoofs on cobbled streets.

Finally, there is a form of vernacular art that, but for the winds of change in farm buildings, might stand forever, and that is the art of the stone mason. The mason's art reaches a peak in many of the barn walls shown in these pages, and, even in a photograph, the eye can take in the sheer beauty of a rubble wall, its colour and texture and the happy arrangement of the stones in their courses. These walls are solid, and their strength is sometimes emphasized by those narrow apertures that are more often found in medieval fortresses. In an age of stone veneer and prefabricated masonry, we shall not see their like again.

c

d

c) A datestone on a barn is a rare and pleasant discovery.

d) The sheaf of wheat in a Victorian brooch made of human hair.

a

b

c

d

a) Around 1827, there was a quality to lettering on barns and tombstones even when done by simple folk. Many had trouble with the letter N and with gauging the length of a line.
Location: near Salisbury, Somerset County, Pennsylvania.

b) The farmer leaves his initials and the date, 1858, for posterity to see.
Location: Markham Township, Ontario.

c) A tablet on the same barn as the illustration above, with the same quality of lettering.

d) Detail of the carved message on the lintel at the beginning of this chapter.
Location: Rockwood, Ontario.

186

e) A lightning rod on a barn in Ontario. The purple glass ball was customarily added to take away from the purely functional appearance of the rod, but, when broken, was an indication to the farmer that lightning had struck.
Location: Moltke, Ontario.

f-h) A trio of vanes: the cock from Ontario, the fish and the beaver from Quebec.

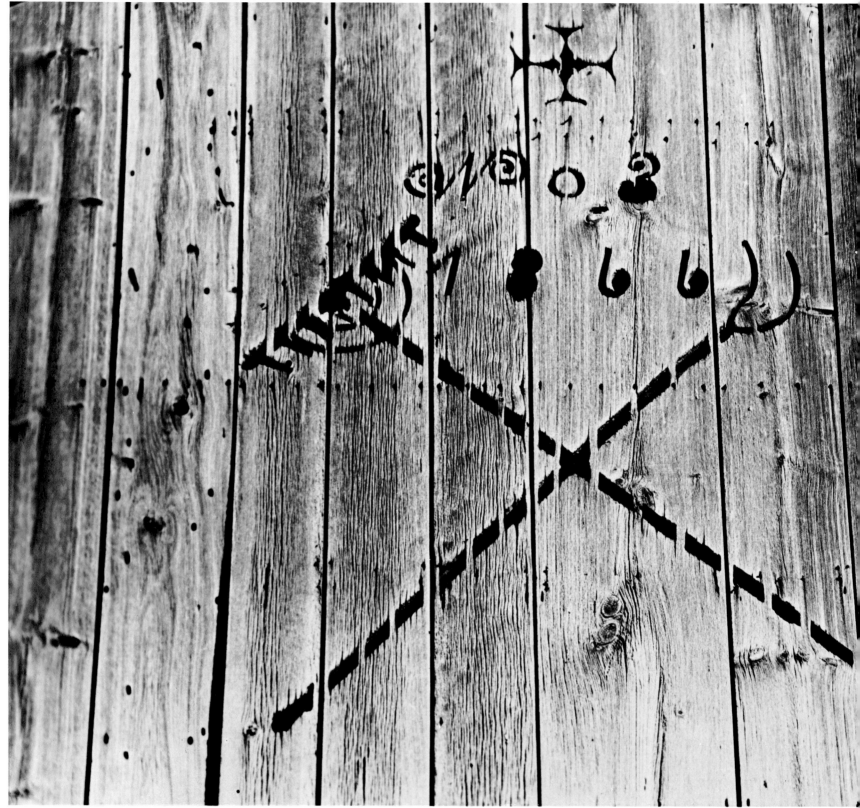

a

a) It is remarkable that so delicate a piece of carving as the rake and the fork should be legible after a century of exposure to the weather. A refinement that did not make the carver's task easier was the strip of the board running through every three inches.
Location: near Maryhill, Ontario.

b

b) View of the rake from inside the barn.

189

The Québecois love colour, and it finds expression on the barn in the painting of the wagon doors in brilliant colours in an infinite variety of designs – the spontaneous creations of the habitant farmer.

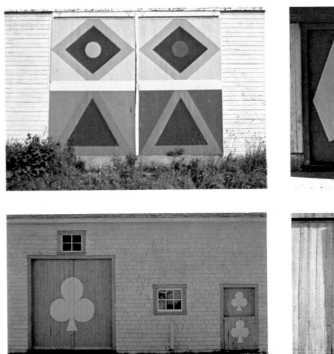

a

b

c

d

a,b) How indebted we are to the farmer who saw his sheep-cote silhouetted against the sky as more than a shelter for sheep. He kept hay in the loft and legend has it that he could watch over his flocks in the fields through a dormer on all four faces. This wonderful little building is near Millpoint in New York State.

c) This seemingly prehistoric object is, actually, an impressive well cover at Carlow, Ontario.

e

f

g

d) A fretwork star on a gable.
Location: near Shanksville, Somerset County, Pennsylvania.

e) Not functional at all are these graceful fretwork panels, which the farmer or his wife must have felt gave interest to an otherwise plain plank wall. The lace-like quality of the panels is given an added interest by the fading paintwork surrounding them.
Location: same as d.

f) Gaiety in the gable.
Location: Edie, Somerset County, Pennsylvania.

g) Whatever one's tastes, one could not begrudge the painter the riot of form and colour that he gave us on this barn gable. The name on the panel, and presumably of the farmer who authorized the decoration, is Blough, 1902.
Location: near Edie, Somerset County, Pennsylvania.

a

b

a, b) Location: Farewell, Ontario.

c

c) In this spirited piece of painting, the quality of drawing approaches the standards of fine art rather than of vernacular which relies so much on the silhouette of horse or cow. Colours are rose, blue, red, and grey, with background of mountains and snow. The mural measures 10' x 8'.
Location: Petit Chocpiele, New Brunswick.

d,e) Horse weathervanes from an old catalogue, with the description "14 x 18 inches, mounted complete as shown above, made of copper and gilded with gold leaf."

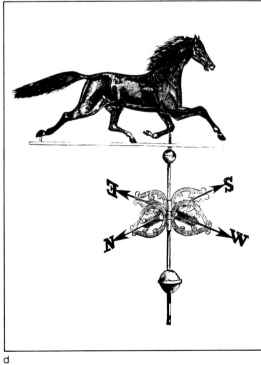

d

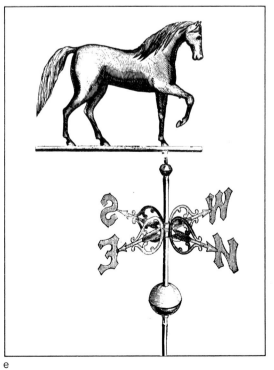

e

a

c

a) The painter who deals in geometric shapes could hardly improve on this scene if he thought in abstract terms. The location of the door is perfect, as are the windows tied to the wall by the equally appropriate little roof. One feels the milk cans could be placed nowhere but where they are, and the horse completes the picture.
Location: Highway 15B, Montmorency County, Quebec.

d

e

f

g

h

b) An admirable example of folk art in a very sophisticated piece of design.
Location: near Woodville, Ontario.

c) Early morning mist on a familiar sign.

d) This fine picture of cattle was painted by the farmer's wife, Mrs. Beulah Pinder. It measures 12' x 24'
Location: Highway 6, north of Mount Forest, Ontario.

e) Draft horses painted over an old cigarette sign.
Location: Chatsworth, Ontario.

f) Location: Highway 89, south of Harriston, Pennsylvania.

g) Location: near Topton, Pa.

h) Location: same as g.

a

b

c

a) The mason's art reaches a peak in many of the barn walls illustrated here, and even in a photograph the eye can take in the sheer beauty of a rubble wall, its colour, texture, and the happy arrangement of the stones in their courses.

b) Novel way of framing embrasure vents by vertical ashlar stones.

c) A doorway in the Kindersley's barn.
Location: north of Ballinafad, Ontario.

d) Not as permanent as masonry, but just as beautiful, is the stovewood wall: laid, perhaps with the help of the whole family. Birch logs of about 16″ in length are set in lime mortar. Because of its instability, the wall is usually reinforced at corners by quoins in brick or stone. This is quite the finest stovewood wall known to the authors, with a wide variety of log ends to add to its charm.

e) This must be one of the few log piggeries extant.
Location: Pioneer Village, Toronto, Ontario.

f) A favourite type of wall where the mortar is generously applied. The pink, blue and other colours in the split glacial boulders shine through. But more important in this picture is the tenant appearing at his private entrance.
Location: Egremont township, Ontario.

g) A longer view of this very substantial piggery, showing other tenants' exits and entrances.

198

d

e

f

g

a

b

c

d

e

a) A fascinating wall, in which the mason makes a striking contrast between his large split boulders and the low random coursing of the wall.
Location: near Uxbridge, Ontario.

b) One can imagine the mason standing back to admire the novel frame he had created for this ventilating slit.
Location: Arkell, Ontario.

c) The picture creates the illusion that the wall is growing from an outcropping of rock at grade level.
Location: near Durham, Ontario.

d) An exceptionally fine barn and equally fine masonry. The pattern of brickwork is the traditional sheaf of wheat with lateral "diamond" additions.
Location: Route 45, near Hereford, Maryland.

e) Where weathered pine planks are invariably grey (and much in demand for atmosphere in recreation rooms and the like), clapboards in the same wood turn brown and silver with age. Here they are fragile and curved with age, but held in place by hand-forged rails.
Location: Mohawk Valley.

f

f) A secluded courtyard with memories of harvests long
past.

Part 4

The Barn in Detail

The blacksmith's work, as with the carpenter's, shows
individuality in both design and craftsmanship.

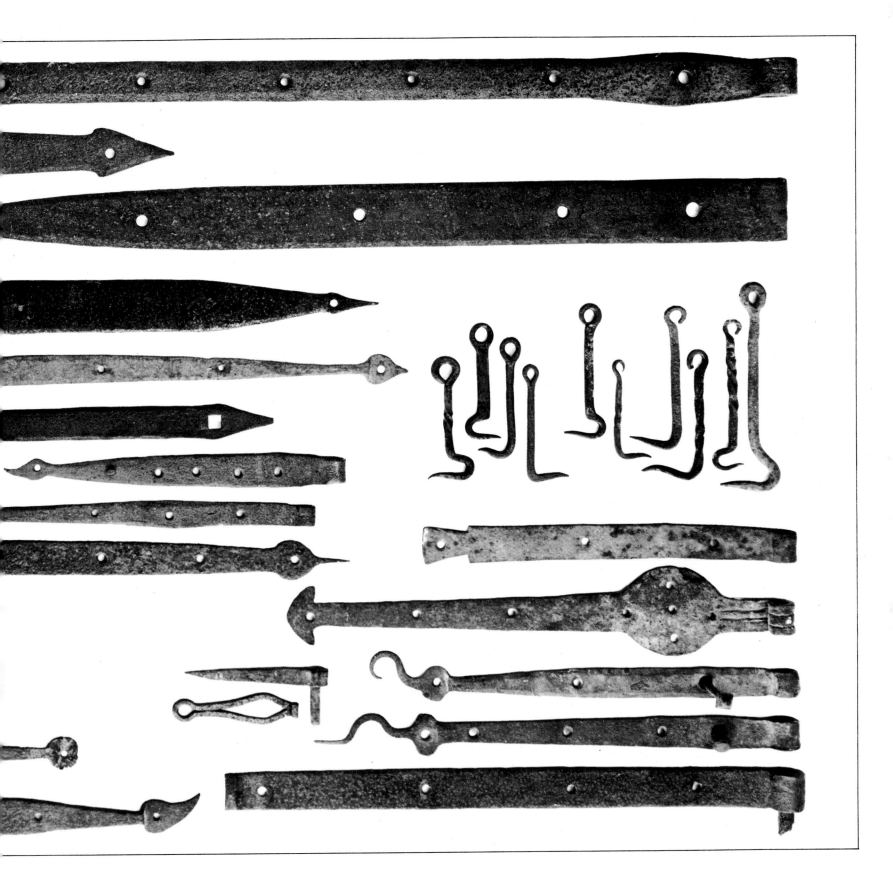

a

a) This contemporary scene near Lindsay, Ontario, could have been observed a century ago before the advent of the binder. The barn is venerable, and the old-fashioned stooks are tied with straw.

b

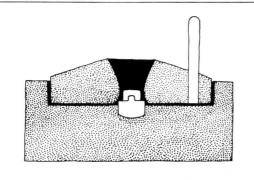

c

d

b) The flail and the winnowing tray are the reminders of bygone harvests. The sheaves on the threshing floor are ready for the flailer.
Location: Black Creek Pioneer Village, Ontario.

c) Cross-section of a quern from Roman Britain.

d) Looking at this implement for grinding corn, we see something that goes back millennia in human history. The story is told that "St. Columba ground his corn in a quern, commencing the hymn *Altus Prosator* as he put the first feed into the hopper of the mill, and finishing the hymn and his grinding simultaneously." That was at Iona in the year 563 AD. The quern in our illustration is in the Black Creek Pioneer Village, Ontario.

Threshing and Winnowing

fig. 1.

Centuries before the barn evolved as a shelter for fodder and animals, there was corn to be threshed and then, so poetic a word, winnowed. Frequent references have been made in these pages to the threshing floor, (or *threshold* to give it its ancient name), and its location in the barn, but the threshing floor of biblical times was an open-air affair with a carefully prepared clay floor–usually a circular enclosure fifty to a hundred feet in diameter on which the sheaves were spread. If the farm were small, the sheaves would be threshed by beating with a stick or cudgel, or, if larger, by drawing oxen, sheep or other animals round and round as they trod the grain with their hoofs–a technique still to be found in undeveloped parts of the world.

Improvements on this method were probably more efficient, but did not dispense with the services of the incontinent ox, and they took the form of a sledge, an artifact that appears through history and makes its final appearance, about 1850, in New York State! The threshing sledge or *charatz* of Egypt and the *morag* of the Hebrews consisted of a heavy frame mounted with three or more rollers, sometimes spiked, which revolved as

The sheaves were opened and piled on the floor for the threshers, whom we see wielding their flails which, like the quern, are among the most ancient implements used in agriculture. Later, the chaff and grain would be put in the winnowing basket and poured in a wind over a sheet on the floor. The chaff was blown over the threshing floor and the grain, being heavier, settled on the sheet. This method was popular in North America, but only one of many in olden times in other parts of the world.

it was drawn over the spread-out sheaves. One of the earliest pieces of humane legislation in the world must have been the prohibition in the Mosaic code that forbade the farmer to muzzle the ox that did the threshing or the one that did the dragging of the spiked frame, so that he could eat his fill as he circled the threshing floor.[1]

References to threshing in the Bible are many, and range all the way from "cudgels" to beat the smaller grains to "machines." Mechanical devices were three: the first a square piece of wood armed on the lower side with sharp stones, and, presumably, dragged over the sheaves; the second, a square frame again, but with iron wheels having teeth like a saw; while the third resembled the second except that the wheels were omitted and six-inch spikes were fastened to the frame.[2] All were heavy and were dragged by oxen over the sheaves.

The Romans in Britain brought with them a threshing implement called a *tribulum* which was a flat sledge of wood, thirty feet square, with the underside furnished with holes into which were inserted flakes or splinters of stone or, sometimes, pieces of iron. A heavy weight was put on the sledge, or was supplied by the weight of the driver standing upon it. Like others of its kind, it was drawn by oxen and may have been a primitive survival from ancient times in Italy and not a new invention.[3] A method still in use in Italy consists of a tapered roller fastened to a pole in the centre of the threshing floor and pulled round at the heavier end by oxen.

Our modern term for such devices would be gadgets, and primitive and inefficient as they were, they were highly productive compared with the method of the Celts in Britain in the fourth century B.C. Like their successors the Romans, the Saxons, Angles and others, they found the climate damp, and their traditional methods of separating the grain from the sheaf unpractical. The Celts developed a technique of their own to meet these new climatic conditions, and what they came up with was so puny, to us so futile, that it makes a fantastic contrast with the million-bushel output of the threshing machines of the Canadian prairies and the American west.

Their method was to burn the husks. Picture a woman holding a handful of corn

a

b

c

a) This rather oriental-looking scene is actually on Prince Edward Island in Canada. Hay is protected by a hipped roof which can be adjusted up or down depending on the height of the stacked hay. It is a technique to be found on the Magdalen Islands as well as in other parts of the world.

b) A silo built of glowing red bricks about the turn of the century. It might well remind some of a minor tower in northern Italy.
Location: New York State.

c) An octagonal silo of well-laid masonry, recalling the Middle Ages rather than a period remembered by many now living.
Location: New York State.

d) A well-worn threshing floor showing heavy boards, three inches thick, splined and pegged to sleepers below.

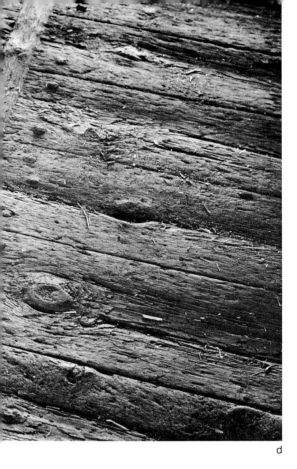

d

by the stalks in her left hand, while at the same time she sets fire to the ears and beats off the grain smartly and quickly with a stick in her right hand. "Corn may thus be dressed, winnowed, ground and baked in an hour."[4] So hard did old customs die in rural Britain that the story of the woman and the burning husks was told by a traveller who saw her at work, not in 400 B.C., but in A.D. 1703 on a farm on one of the western isles of Scotland.[5]

With time, the Celtic farms increased in size and more efficient methods of threshing than burning by hand became necessary. This was achieved by the development of a kiln, a covered structure where the sheaves could be held and threshed over a fire.[6] A surprising feature of the kiln was its occasional considerable size, like the one at Iona which was large enough for storage with a central space for threshing. The King's kiln in the Welsh laws was used as a lodging place for his huntsmen who would lie warm and dry on the unthreshed corn. There were, too, the usually sensible laws and bylaws such as the ones that forbade the kiln or the smithy in the hamlet to be closer than nine paces to the nearest house.

In the north of England in the Middle Ages there were charming little buildings curiously named "gin gangs," actually covered unheated threshing houses. They were octagonal in plan with a huge central post and a timbered roof supported on stone columns. The sides were open. Miss Cook writes that "these buildings have the same relation to the barn as the baptistery to the cathedral."[7]

Beating sheaves with a stick or cudgel must antedate all other methods of threshing. It was followed by the flail, an instrument so effective and so simple in construction that it continued in universal use from remote times to the twentieth century.[8] The word comes from the Latin *flagellum,* the root of "flagellant," and in the heat of summer the flailer must have been conscious of the similarity of his task and the self imposed torture of the flagellant of his time. A man in good health was able to give the sheaves thirty to forty strokes or blows a minute and his output for the day would average eight bushels of wheat, thirty bushels of oats, eight of rye, or twenty of buckwheat.[9]

Did Ruth "when sick for home...amid the alien corn" use stick or cudgel? We do not know, but Boaz permitted her to "glean even among the sheaves" and, so "until even," she "beat out that she had gleaned, and it was about an ephah of barley."[10]

Only the threshing machine, the product of the industrial revolution, replaced the flail, but its use lingers on in isolated small farms and primitive communities in various parts of the world. "It consisted of two pieces of wood, the handstaff and the beater fastened together loosely at one end by a thong of raw hide or eel skin. The handstaff is a light rod of ash, about five feet long, heavier at one end where it is pierced by a thong which binds it to the beater or swingle. The latter is a wooden rod thirty inches long made of ash, or, better, of thorn: it is cylindrical of about 1¼″ diameter, and constructed so that the edge of the grain received the force of the blow. Some carefully made flails had a wooden swivel attached to the handle to prevent kinking and twisting of the thong. It will be clear from the shape and construction of the flail that a man could stand in an upright position and pound the sheaves on the floor at his feet."[11]

The thong on the flail wore out rapidly and was the one weak spot in the contrivance. The most durable material ever found for this purpose was eel skin, and, says the author of "Threshing" in *The Golden Age of Homespun,* "I can remember when two or three skins were nailed up in the barn ready for use, and there they remained for years after the flail had been laid away forever."[12] Writing of his farm memories as a boy in New York State, he goes on to say: "So far as I can learn oats, barley and buckwheat were generally threshed under the feet of horses, but wheat, rye and peas were flailed. During the first half of last century, a considerable acreage of wheat was grown on my family's farm each year, and, until about 1850, it was beaten out with flails. Wheat is hard to thresh and needs pounding to clear the grain from the straw. It must be fully ripened, and, sometimes was exposed to rain before drawing in though I never heard of that particular bit of farm practice from anyone except my father."[13]

"The use of the flail for threshing rye was kept up long after it had been discontinued for other purposes. For one thing, rye threshes more easily than other grain. More

a

important was the fact that rye straw had a special sales value for making old fashioned brown paper and for other uses, but this value was conditional on the straw being straight and unbroken and bound in bundles. The sheaves of rye were unbound and laid on the floor in two rows, the heads overlapping and the butts outward. The two flailsmen worked systematically over them, striking alternately in the same spot and beating a rhythmic tattoo. The straw was then turned over so as to present a fresh surface and the process repeated until the grain was beaten out. When finished, the chaff and grain were carefully shaken, and the straw straight and unbroken was rebound by hand, a process that to us seems incredibly laborious."[14]

The same author remembers a John Brown who died at ninety after working the best part of sixty years on his farm. He and another man used to work together and flail out rye "for the tenth bushel." They would each do ten bushels a day at a time when rye was worth seventy-five cents, and their individual pay of one dollar was considered "a satisfactory wage for a winter's day a century

b

c

a) The successor to the flail— the steam-driven threshing machine.

b) An old threshing floor in a log crib barn. Location: Black Creek Pioneer Village, Ontario.

c) A four-horsepower machine, used to drive a threshing machine. Location: same as *b*.

ago." Grain flailed easiest on snapping cold days, but there was little hardship involved, for it was work at which a man had no difficulty in keeping warm, and was regarded as pleasant employment in rough weather.[15] It was customary for the thresher with a flail to wear shoes made from an old hat so as not to bruise the grain, but we read of no such precaution for the hoofs of horses or oxen engaged in a similar task. It is worth noting that in the mid-nineteenth century in New York State, the ancient tenth bushel crops up again in the history of the barn, but in a more democratic age the farm labourer was the recipient and not the parson or the lord of the manor.

But whether the threshing was done by the plodding tread of animal's hoofs, by sledge or cylinder, or by flail, the grain still had to be separated from the chaff. It had to be winnowed, and we get a clue to its origin in the Old English word *windwian* meaning a wind. It is generally agreed that with all peoples in all ages until our own, winnowing was dependent on a favourable breeze. All old English and many North American barns were so placed that the prevailing wind blew through the threshing floor from open doors at one end to a winnowing window or open doors at the other. Thus Daniel the prophet, when he wished to convey the idea of the utter destruction and dispersal of the image with its head of gold and feet of iron and clay, declared that the pieces became "like the chaff of the summer threshing floors: and the wind carried them away."[16] Shakespeare is even more precise when he says in Henry IV, "We shall be winnowed by so rough a wind that even our corn shall seem as light as chaff and good from bad find no partition."

Sometimes the grain and chaff were tossed – the chaff being carried on the breeze while the grain fell to the floor. This, in England was regarded as a simple method of grading as the heavier grain would fall nearer to the tosser while the lighter would fall farther away. Nearer home, there was John Sharpe of New York State, who remembers his grandmother and grandfather standing on the barn floor with the big doors open on each side and holding aloft a tray from which they shook the contents, chaff and grain, gradually over the edge. The wind did the rest.

In mid-nineteenth-century Ontario there were still farmers who were as truly pioneers as any south of the line who may have settled in the eighteenth century. Mr. John McDonald was one and, in writing of winnowing, he refers to a "wecht," a tray that was made up of a sheepskin with wool removed, tacked, but not stretched, to a wooden rim. The tray was used as a scoop to lift the grain and chaff, after which it was poured in the wind over a sheet on the floor. He tells of a grim day in his life on that Ontario farm when his family was without flour and he, desperate man, was without wind. But a breeze came up at sundown, and, so dire were the family straits, that he kept at work by the light of the moon till two in the morning. He had already spent a full day threshing by flail, and the dawn saw him "off with my grain to the Harris's Mill twenty miles away."[17] The year was 1854.

Countless farmers throughout history have known the frustration and anxiety of an airless day and failing light with chaff and grain at their feet, waiting to be winnowed. It would seem so obvious that where nature failed to produce a draft, a man with a helper could do so quite effectively with a fan. References are few on the subject, but M. E. Seebohm writes of a wicker fan which was supplanted by the sail fan. The latter was composed of slats arranged in a cylindrical form with a piece of sacking attached as a sail to each slot. This needed three men – one to turn the fan, one to heave the corn and one to fill the riddle or coarse sieve for the grain.[18] The wicker fan would seem to require no explanation, and as with the story of so many ancient and primitive implements, it is necessary to fall back on the Bible, where John the Baptist speaks of one: "whose fan is in his hand and he will thoroughly purge his floor, and gather his wheat into the garner; but he will burn up the chaff with unquenchable fire."[19]

The arrival of the winnowing machine, the fanning mill of the future, was inevitable. It came from China where it was used in the "cleaning" of rice. From China, it reached Holland, it crossed the channel to Scotland through the agency of Andrew Fletcher of Saltoun (1655–1716) a Scottish patriot of extraordinarily wide interests of whom the *Dictionary of National Biography* says he introduced from Holland "an improved barley mill and fanners." Among other things, Fletcher of Saltoun was a diplomat and

soldier and unlikely, personally, to have put his mill and fanners into production. In fairness, he should share the distinction with James Meikle, the so-called "inventor of the winnowing machine" in the year 1720.

Nothing could demonstrate better the slow evolution of tools or machines for threshing than the fact that one can leap through time from Roman Britain at the beginning of the Christian era to New York State in the nineteenth century, and see no noticeable change in threshing technique. Many of our old barns were framed with one or two giant "swing beams," timbers of unbelievable size sometimes two feet in depth and forty feet long. They were designed to "carry the heavy overhead mows without any central support, and thus leave a clear unobstructed floor. In the middle of this a small post was set up and a light sweep attached to serve as a guide for the horses which were driven in a circle round it, often with merriment and a crack of the whip. Meanwhile, men kept turning over the sheaves and shaking out the grain and chaff. Horses were unshod and oxen were often used."[20]

Later, someone devised the "wooden nigger." "This was simply a log ten feet or twelve feet long with many auger holes into which stout wooden pegs were driven. One end of this was pivoted to a central post while a team hooked to the free end drew it around and around like the sweep of an old fashioned hay press. As the team made their rounds, the 'nigger' bumped and rolled behind them and doubtless added greatly to their efficiency.' So primitive was this implement that a first-century Roman reincarnated as a farmhand in New York State would have played a part unchanged in the intervening years.

The evolution of the threshing machine, with or without the capability of winnowing in the same operation, seems to have developed in Scotland. In 1732, Michael Menzies designed a machine that consisted of a series of flails drawn by a water wheel. In 1758, Stirling of Dunbane invented a thresher on the principle of the flax mill, and James Sharpe, unadorned by any fine place name like Dunbane, is remembered for a winnowing machine that cleaned and sorted grain.

We come finally in Scotland to Andrew Meikle, a namesake, probably, of the James

Meikle who developed the Sino-Dutch model of the winnowing machine. According to the *Dictionary of National Biography,* Andrew Meikle (1719–1811) first appears as the inventor of a threshing machine that proved unsuccessful in 1778, but was followed by one eight years later which is generally regarded as the forerunner of all threshing machines, and the first practical thresher. The dictionary adds a melancholy note to his obituary – a subscription was raised for him in 1809, his ninetieth year.

Contrary to what one would expect, the United States in the early days showed nothing like the activity of Scotland in labour-saving threshing machines. Van Wagenen refers to a Scottish invention of 1732 "where bye one man can do as much work as six men here to fore,"[21] but for that American historian, the invention of the real modern thresher took place on the day that "a man bethought him of a swiftly revolving drum with metal teeth – an epoch-making idea which is said to be a strictly American conception." No monument from a grateful nation marks his grave any more than Andrew Meikle's, but in this case even the name is lost to posterity. Legend or fact, this shadowy figure was a "New Hampshire Yankee who migrated to Saratoga County New York, and brought with him in his wagon, or perhaps in his head, a threshing machine embodying the great idea."[22] We do know that such a revolutionary machine based on the "great idea" was developed by T. D. Burrall, a farmer-mechanic of Geneva, New York, who in about 1830 was able to put it on the market.

The first machines "were nothing more than a cylinder and without any provision for separating the straw from the chaff and grain, but compared with former methods they were a revolutionary advance. The first source of power was the sweep power with from two to six horses, but about 1840 the tread horsepower came in." That they saved time over flailing was irrefutable, but they were far more efficient, and it is difficult to picture a situation in the middle of the Industrial Revolution where the highest achievement of the machine was a disheartening heap of straw, chaff and grain – all of which had to be sorted by hand. A giant step forward was the addition of a shaker, which allowed the chaff and grain to fall unham-

a

a) These faintly scribed tally marks recall the day when
the flailers kept their count in bushels of threshed
grain.

213

pered by the presence of the straw.

Mr. Young, an Ontario farmer, tells of using a "buzzer threshing machine" until after the turn of the century. This was a permanent fixture of the barn and was located in the mow above the granary. It was driven by four to five teams of horses (Clydesdales) working in a covered shed connected to the machine by a tumbling rod. The threshing machine had a combine separator and the grain spilled into the granary below. It was custom-built by a Mr. Ferguson in his workshop half a mile from the barn. Mr. Young recalls that a threshing outfit came around in the fall. It consisted of a steam traction engine and separator or threshing machine: two men came with the outfit, the engineer and the feeder. The farmer supplied the rest of the labour about fifteen men in all: the machine was fed from the mow, some would stack the straw and two men would collect the grain in bushel baskets and carry them to the bins in the granary.

While the "Saratoga" man, like Piltdown, will always be anonymous, "Agricola," a contributor to the *Cultivator,* was a real person known at any rate to his editor, and Van Wagenen recognized him from his writings as a "scholar and a gentleman." In 1849, he wrote at length of the advantages of the new machine for cleaning and threshing wheat at a time when there was no shortage of labour in Seneca County. His carefully kept books give an illuminating account of the economic climate of his day, and equally illuminating is his willingness to publish, even anonymously, what seems to us so medieval and parsimonious a reward to his serfs. To his credit, he served himself as another "labourer in the vineyard" at a comparable wage. Following is his record of a day's threshing:

One man to feed the machine at 39¢ per day
One man to supply the feeder at 38¢ per day
One man to pitch from the mow at 34¼¢ per day
One man to deliver the straw at 32¢ per day
One man to attend the fanning at 32¢ per day
One man to mill, generally done by self, at 50¢ per day
Total cost of labour per day: $1.93½
For horse and driver: $2.50 per day

Assuming 200 bushels per day (and it could be more), "Agricola" would arrive at a cost per bushel of 2.0021 cents.

Outside the scope of this book is the ulti-mate lot of the grain, its conversion into flour except as it was done by an ancient artifact of great interest. Not as ancient as the flail, but antedating the arrival of the Romans in Britain, was the quern, the primitive mill for grinding corn. It consisted of two flat circular stones: the lower, often shaped with a rim, has a wooden or metal pin in the centre which passes through a hole in the upper stone. The worker pours the grain through the upper hole, while with the other he revolves the upper stone by means of a peg or short post fixed to one side.

Under Welsh law, when a husband and wife separated, the husband took the upper stone and his wife the lower. This would seem to render both useless except, as M. E. Seebohm suggests, the querns of a tribe were much the same size, and if husband and wife entered a new union, they could fit their stone to that of the new partner. The same authority tells the story that St. Columba ground his corn in a quern, commencing the hymn *Altus Prosator* as he put the first feed into the hopper of the mill, and finishing the hymn and his grinding simultaneously.[23]

Throughout history the quern has, generally, been the property of humble folk. For those who could afford it there were, even in Saxon times, tidal mills, water mills, and horse mills where water was not available for grinding corn. By the end of the twelfth century, a new feature in milling appeared with the introduction of the windmill.[24] Refinements and improvements were to follow, but the use of the quern persisted through medieval times and beyond.

Of the many surprises in the search that went into this book, none was more exciting than the discovery of a quern in Ontario in 1970. It is more than likely that the Jesuit martyrs, Fathers Lalement and Brébeuf used a quern when they came to Quebec in 1649, and it is certain that its design was identical with the one over which St. Columba sang at Iona in 536. Among the products of human hands that have remained unchanged through the millennia, none are more remarkable than the flail and the quern. They remained unchanged because, like the axe and the wheel, they had reached a stage of perfection in a primitive society upon which the inventive genius of later generations was unable to improve.

Omnium Gatherum

The following illustrations all relate to the barn but not all to the categories in the rest of the book. Because of their individual interest they are included in this section. The photographs that introduce these pages are taken from a film of a barn raising at Woodbridge, Ontario in 1918.

Barn raising *The following account of a Mennonite barn-raising bee was written by Miss Blodwen Davies in 1960.*
The community bee is a traditional factor in Mennonite life, and can be traced at least as far back as when persecuted family groups of primitive Christians, originally Celts from the Po Valley, were driven back for safety and secrecy to remote uplands in the deep valleys of the Alps, lands which had never been claimed by anyone else. In early spring when cattle were to be driven up to the high meadows there were roads to be rebuilt, herdsmen's cabins to be repaired, and so on, and the community worked as a social unit. The tradition of mutual aid made them excellent settlers in North America, self-reliant, ingenious and thankful for good land and freedom to go their own ways and live their own simple and harmless lives. Their preachers were elected by lot, in accordance with biblical custom, and their only ambition was to live quietly as a brotherhood.
In spite of inevitable modernization affecting their economic life, the Mennonites and other Plain Folks rely on the Bee for a great many community activities. But the really great barn-raising bees are becoming infrequent. The timbers required for a traditional barn are almost unobtainable, except at prohibitive cost, and new ideas in the building and use of barns have affected even Mennonite agricultural life....

In September 1960, she attended a barn raising on a farm where the barn had been destroyed by fire.
...It had belonged to a family named Martin at Floradale. These were Old Order Mennonites who do not believe in carrying insurance on their properties. So when the barn burned, with the loss of the harvested crop and of many animals, the loss was a total loss. However, all communities of Plain Folks cross the lines of sectarian belief in time of trouble. There are Disaster Committees set up in every such community. Without hesitation the whole Mennonite Community, reinforced

a

b

a) On a morning start, neighbours are seen carrying hewn timbers, all of which are numbered. Plates and girts go first to the barn foundation, followed by cross beams and posts.

b) Lifting the timbers and laying them out on the barn floor for the bents.

c

d

f

g

c) Beginning of the raising of the first bent. The width of the ramp indicates a double threshing floor. Women spectators carry umbrellas to protect them from the summer sun.

d) The boss carpenter demands unison in the lifting of the pike poles by the crew and achieves it by his yell of ''Ya–he!'' After each lift, the pike poles are lowered to their next position with the order ''lower–one at a time.'' The pike poles varied in length from ten to thirty feet.

e) The post riders go up with the bent. Their job was gradually to lower the pikes as the bent got higher. Two spectators will be seen precariously perched on the windmill. It has been estimated that 4,000 feet of rope would be used in a bee.

f) The first bent is in position and steadied with ropes and poles until the second bent is up and the two can be connected by girts, braced, and pinned.

g) As a plate is being fitted to the corner post with its brace, the steadying rope can be seen. All this is taking place twenty feet or more above the ground.

h) The ladder on the bent would suggest its traditional position on the threshing floor. The purlin has been fitted. Activity here has to do with the arrival of the main plate to be fitted and the driving-in of pins.

e

h

i

by many of their non-Mennonite neighbours, went into action. The fire occurred on a Tuesday night and burned on into Wednesday morning, September 21. On the tenth day later, October 1, the new barn was erected. Forty to fifty men had worked each day but Sunday in the intervening time. They cleared up the debris of the barn, stables, and big chicken house, reinforced old foundations and built new ones, and built a cement block milk house attached to the barn. They had gone into another part of the county, dismantled two pioneer barns that had stood for a century or more, and hauled the timbers with teams to the site of the new barn. These were horse-and-buggy people, and though they used tractors in some cases, their main source of power was still horse-power. One team of horses was killed in an accident in the course of the preparatory work while hauling some of these timbers.

Meantime the women and girls had also moved in, in daily teams, to prepare meals for the workers. They took with them vegetables and apples to fill temporary bins built in the basement of the house, where much of the work was done. In one corner hung a great collection of smoked hams, and various kinds of smoked meats, some of them a yard long and five inches in diameter, along with fresh meat and sausages. With the efficiency of generations of experience, the women organized themselves according to need, some looking after the preparation of vegetables, some looking after pies, cakes, cookies, breads and buns. In one corner a great area of floor was covered with bottles of canned fruits, beets, pickles, and spiced sauces. Tables and shelves were improvised, and the foods prepared for serving. Among other stoves in use was one in the summer kitchen called the kettle stove. This consists of a big cylindrical stove with the fire fed through a door at floor level, and set into the cylinder was a thirty-gallon saucepan. This kind of stove has many uses, but in this case meat stews were cooked in it and on the day of the raising it was full of stewed beef in rich gravy.

All this work was most cheerfully done and there was a sort of festival air, an opportunity for the kind of community gathering which all the Plain Folks love. They do not have parties, but any occasion which is a legitimate occasion for working together or for worshipping together is welcomed as a

j

i) Two more bents are about to rise, with upwards of two hundred men on the barn floor. The barn was approximately 134 feet in length.

j) Rafters are on the ground waiting to be fitted, Two men can be seen walking on the plate high above the crowd on the floor.

k

l

time to exchange news and to break bread together. Consequently the atmosphere at any kind of bee is genuinely hospitable, lively, and happy.

Anyone who came to the barn raising was made welcome at the outdoor meal. Fortunately the October day was a perfect specimen of an Ontario autumn day, sunny and warm. Some men, probably beyond the age for barn raising activity, went to work setting up tables and benches between the house and the orchard. They carried in cement blocks and long planks and set places for just over a hundred people.

Then the women set the tables and loaded them with food. Under some trees, tubs of water were set for the men's washing-up and presently hats were hung on the trees, along with a line for towels, as the men scrubbed up for dinner.

All the labour was voluntary and unpaid. The only man to receive a nominal fee for his service was the master carpenter with special skills as a barn builder. He gave up other paid work without question to take on the emergency work.

One interesting factor in this group effort is the minimum of orders given. These men have worked at so many barn raisings—except for the very young–and each seems to know where to fall into place.

On this occasion one team of men started putting on the siding before the beams and rafters were all in place. Some of them were anxious to begin work on the roof. But here the father of the young farmer who owned the barn stepped in. He refused to let his neighbours begin the roof work in the later part of the afternoon when many of them were tired from the long day's exertions. This, he told me, was when accidents happened. So, because of common sense and consideration, a limit was put to the day's accomplishment and the whole of the great event passed off happily without an accident of any kind.

Barn-building skills are becoming more and more rare. The cost of building a barn comparable to the old pioneer barn is prohibitive. The settler had his rock for foundations and his pine trees for timbers on his own land. The pooled knowledge and skill of his neighbours provided traditional plans and workmanship. Today the cost of suitable timbers and hired workmen put the cost

k) The last task is the framing of the rafters.

l) But the final act in the performance is supper, the responsibility of the farmer/owner. Though the practice was discouraged in some barn raisings, the men who finished their job of rafters first had prior place at the supper table. This was of some importance, as the meal for so many men had to be held in shifts.

a

Barefaced Tenon A tenon with a single shoulder. (The wall studs in the barn are usually bareface.)

Basilican Plan The basilican plan was devised originally in remote times for barns where the span was too great for rafters to take the load of the roof, and too wide for horizontal beams, if they could be found, to tie the outer walls at the level of the plate. The purlin, in the framework of the barn, is a longitudinal member that supports the rafters at mid-length between the plate and the ridge, and the posts that were introduced support the purlin.

The result was a central space known by historians as the *nave* and a gallery at the sides forming an *aisle*. In the earliest examples known, this arrangement was formed on the ground floor of the barn-the nave was the threshing floor and the aisles were fitted up as stalls for animals over which were "mezzanines" where men and women farm workers slept.

In the eighteenth and nineteenth centuries, the Dutch barns of New York State followed this ancient custom, except for the mezzanines for male and female labourers. It was followed in some circular barns, notably the Shaker barn at Hancock, Mass., but in the banked barn of Pennsylvania, only the form is there: cattle are on the ground floor, and where nave and aisles occur on the floor above, the latter is a gallery used as drive floor and for the storage of vehicles.

Bay The bay in its architectural sense goes back more than two thousand years. It is a term quite unrelated to bay windows or oriels, and describes the spacing of arches in the cathedrals of the Middle Ages, the intervals between steel columns in a modern office building, or between posts in a barn.

Beam Originally, "the squared timber of a whole tree."

Beetle or **Maul** A heavy wooden mallet usually having iron reinforcing hoops or rings on the head designed to pound beams into place.

Bent The prefabricated framed unit of a barn which forms the bays. Bents are perhaps the most recognizable feature of the work of the

beyond the reach of the average farmer. Pole barns and other types of manufactured barn materials are making the old-fashioned barn a subject for folklore.

The folklore of the pioneer, so long ignored in many parts of North America, will some day be recognized as a rich heritage of human values, courage, ingenuity, neighbourliness, and a love of freedom genuine enough to be paid for in physical effort, and in faith, hope and charity.

Courtesy of the Department of Archives, Province of Ontario

a) The interior of the ring barn at Shelburne, Vermont, looking toward the silos.

b

c

d

e

individual barn framer or carpenter. In the raising "bee," they were erected one after the other, being mortised in the sill and connected by the plate, with the girts all made rigid by braces.

Blind Mortise A rectangular slot that is not cut right through the timber, and which receives a stub tenon.

Boring Machine A tool used for drilling the pin and mortise holes. The operator sat astride the timber and used both arms to work the crank handle for boring.

Breeding or Ring Barn at Shelburne, Vermont This type of barn fits none of the categories used in this book, but it is so outstanding for its size, its date (1892), and the quality of its construction that it finds a place in this section. It was built by Dr. William Seward Webb "to house and train the hackney horses which he was attempting to introduce to America." The barn is 418' x 107', and the exercise ring is 370' x 85'. There are 32 box stalls around the ring and 22 on one end, each measuring 12' x 16'. The ten stalls at the other end measure 20' x 20'. The entrance doorway was large enough to admit a road coach and passengers.

The silos are an addition made necessary for a modern cattle-breeding program. If anything, they add to the scale of the interior, and give it, in certain lights, an almost Piranesi atmosphere.

The architect was Robert Henderson Robertson (1829-1919).

Brickwork The beauty of a brick wall comes from several things-colour, texture, the colour and thickness of the mortar, how truly it is laid both vertically and horizontally, and the size of the bricks and their arrangement in courses. This last is called *bond,* and of the many kinds of bond used in brickwork two are practically universal in barns. They are common or English bond, in which a row of headers (the brick ends) occur every sixth or seventh course, and Flemish, in which headers follow stretchers in every course. The stability which bond gives to the wall comes from the headers, which lock into the mortar of the wall four inches (or a fraction more) behind the rear face of the stretchers. How important it is can be demonstrated by a wall of stretchers with-

b) Early photograph of the same barn, showing panelled walls and horses standing outside their stalls.

c) Common bond.

d) Flemish bond.

e) Exterior of the ring barn at Shelburne, showing cupolas and other sources of light.

a

b

out headers: it is then a mere veneer of brick-work, usually strengthened by flat metal ties embedded in the mortar behind the bricks. The majority of brick barns are found in Pennsylvania. The bricks follow the standard American dimension of 2¼″ x 3¾″ x 8″, though exceptional examples exist in early barns of a larger brick, 2½″ x 4½″ x 9¼″.

Clapboarding Known also as weather boarding, clapboarding is the sheathing or clothing for the barn or house. It is always horizontal and always lapped. It is to be found on every type of structure whether it be square, polygonal or circular. It is best known on rectangular barns and least common on circular. Two things are important in an examination of an old clapboarded barn: the amount of lap (which is not easily seen), and the amount of board that is exposed to the weather. The dimensions of the exposed board vary from four to eight inches. The board is usually tapered; that is, thicker at the butt (the exposed part) than at the top. In early buildings it was of even thickness throughout, like a plank. Generally speaking, the older the barn the narrower the board, and because of the problems inherent in curvature the boards in the circular barn are always narrow. Several barns have been examined in this study where they were so old as to be concave, and their exposed bottom edges were paper thin.
In domestic architecture horizontal boards may be flush, i.e. without lap, and they may also be tongued and grooved and V-jointed, but such treatment must be rare in barn construction. However, not at all uncommon in barns of this century is the board and battened barn where the boards are vertical and butt, and the "joint" is covered by a vertical batten. Such a barn admits no ventilation by shrinkage: adequate louvered panels and possibly a cupola must be provided.

Clerestory Usually a wall rising above an aisle roof in church or barn with evenly spaced windows. In such a situation, the building may be rectangular, circular, or polygonal. (The barn at Hancock is a good example.) It may also refer to a lantern sitting squarely on the ridge and giving light to the mow.

Cruck A very early system of timber framing in which a pair of tree trunks roughly trimmed of their branches, and, so bent by nature that,

a) The five bents can be clearly defined silhouetted against the sky in a barn raising at Floradale, Ontario.

b) This horse-driven machine was used to move frame barns on rollers to new locations. With leverage on the shaft and the mechanical advantage of block and tackle, the encircling horse gave ample power to move the building slowly but surely. Sturdy chains anchored the capstan.

c

when brought together, they formed a curved Λ. With one pair of crucks at the end of the barn (or house) and another at the other, the two were braced by a ridge pole. The curved walls were filled with a network of sticks which formed a bond for mud or plaster-an ancient building technique commonly called "wattle and daub", "cob", or *"en torchis."*

Cupola A small domed structure, often one of several on a Renaissance church, or one of many on a Russian cathedral. Almost always it plays a subordinate part to the great dome, the scale of which is enhanced by its presence. On the barn there may be one or two, and rarely more. They are not built of stone like their namesakes in ecclesiastical structures, but are universally of wood. Like its prototype, the cupola may be there to admit light to the space below, but quite often its function is ventilation. In plan, it may be square, circular, or polygonal, and depending on its use, its fenestration may consist of louvres or windows. Many appear in this book, but a striking one has been saved for this page. It is to be found, if years of neglect and the coming winter do not take their toll, on Highway 12 in Ontario. It was a lonely road indeed in the nineteenth century when the barn was built, according to local story, by an eccentric Englishman. It is a roomy cupola, and he is said to have taken his ease in it while, with a megaphone, he exhorted the labourers in the fields to greater efforts.
On the same barn, and known to generations of architectural students is a window, the prototype for which is to be seen on the famous villa at Vicenza by Palladio. The same window is well known on Boodles Club on St. James Street in London, and on the Earl of Burlington's villa at Chiswick, but those are very different buildings from the present ruined barn in Ontario. Research may find that the sitter in the cupola was a traveller who brought the sketch book he filled as a young man on the grand tour of Europe to the construction of his barn in far-off rural Ontario. It is a pleasure to record it here, even though one cannot think it served any purpose in the mow except when it was empty, and then but little.

Dormer The dormers or windows in a roof are better known on the house than on the barn. They are not common in the latter for

d

e

c) Location: near Coldwater, Ontario.

d) A glazed cupola,
Location: Bellwood Lake, Ontario.

e) The "Church Farm" barn, so called because of the apparent ecclesiastical appearance of the cupola.
Location: Enosburg, Vermont.

223

a

b

c

the simple reason of their inaccessibility from the mow floor. They were, obviously, not put there for aesthetic considerations, but as sources of light they were not effective when the mow was full, and as ventilators they operated only after the glass in their windows was broken. Double hung or casement dormers suggest a naïvety on the part of the nineteenth-century farmer that is quite likeable, but he must soon have realized the futility of his decision to use either.

In nearly all cases, the dormer is built of wood, and its roof either gabled or hipped. It may be bold and striking on the barn roof, like the one on the Jesuit Mission at Midland, or modest like that uncommon example near Lindsay, Ontario, where the roof is but a continuation of the upper slope of the main gambrel.

Drawbore A technique used by the carpenter to firmly secure the tenoned beam to the mortised post. This was achieved by drilling the pin holes of each piece ⅛″ off centre, so that when the pin was hammered in, the tenon would be "drawn" tightly into the mortise.

Forked Tenon A joint used in framing where a tenon is cut approximately ten inches from the end of the beam and fitted into an open mortise atop the post.

Frame Barn A barn in which the structure is composed of timber members connected by mortise and tenon or halved joints, and covered by boards.

Gain The notch sawn in the mortised member to receive the tenoned member.

Girt The intermediate beam or beams tying the posts between the plate and sill.

Granary In historic times the granary was usually a substantial building of stone, raised on columns with flaired heads to discourage rats and mice. Rodents are still a menace wherever grain is stored, but kept under control by cats and owls. In the New Kingdom of Egypt (1567-1320 B.C.) granaries were small oasthouse-like structures in the courtyard of a gentleman's estate. They were fed through a hole at the top, and the grain was removed at a shuttered port at the foot. The cat in those far-off days was used for hunting

a) The hay rack suspended from the rack lifter.

b) Another illustration of the rack lifter and hay rack, from a different view.

c) The hay door is large enough for the hay to be lifted by the fork before the invention of the hay baler and the compact bale of hay. The totem-like ladder on the pole gave support and access to the hay carrier.

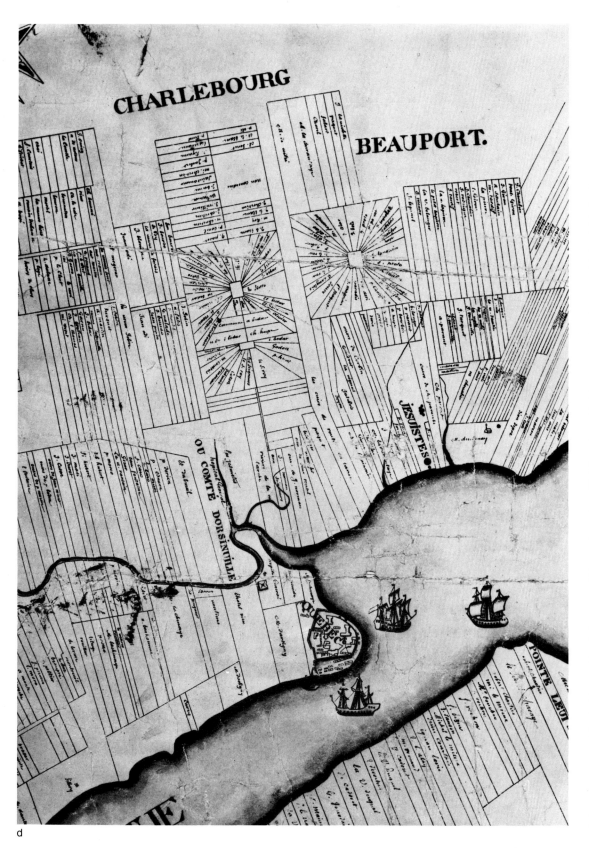

CHARLEBOURG

BEAUPORT.

OU COMTE DORSINTILLE

JÉSUISTES

POINTE LEO

d

d) Early eighteenth-century map showing the long,
narrow family farm lots characteristic of Quebec.

and was far from being domesticated: the substitute for the mouser was snakes, which led
protected lives near the granaries.

In his book *Les Granges du Quebec,* Robert
Séguin shows the plan of an old barn in which
bins for grain, about 3'0" high, flank the
threshing floor. Such a system seems no longer
to exist anywhere in North America, and the
granary, usually at the end of the threshing
floor furthest from the wagon doors, consists
of a series of small rooms facing each other
with adjustable fronts. Our illustration is of
one where the builder, seeking perhaps to em-
phasize the importance of the grain in the farm
economy, has given the bins or cubicles the
architectural treatment of an arcade. (See
page 56.)

Hay Door The opening, usually in the gable
end for the loading of hay from the outside
of the barn into the mow. This door was made
necessary by the widespread use of the mechanical hay fork and hay carrier.

Hay Rack A detachable frame designed to
hold and carry a wagon load of hay from the
field to the barn. (See *rack lifter.*)

Jack Arch A flat arch.

Land Pattern of the Province of Quebec
Several factors were responsible for the unique
pattern in the map of 1709 on this page. They
were in fact three: (1) Settlement was strung
out along the mighty St. Lawrence River, from
the earliest days the great waterway both to
the sea and to the Great Lakes region. (2) The
most fertile available land was a strip lying
between the river and the rocky Laurentian
Shield, and individual settlers were each given
a waterfront. (3) Due to a tradition of multiple
inheritance, farms were divided physically
between surviving sons. Increased population
in primarily agricultural communities over
the centuries put further pressure on the land;
hence the lots on the plan are of incredible
narrowness and end in a point. Several of the
barns in the chapter on Quebec were found
in this area.

Ledged and Braced Door A medieval door
type, and the most commonly used on barns
and outbuildings.

Masonry In practice, building in stone and

building in brick come under the heading of masonry, but here the two crafts are separated as they are in most dictionaries. In any case, the craftsmen are not the same.

Rubble In the lay mind, especially since the bombing of cities in the last war, "rubble" has come to mean a pile of stones, a fallen wall. However, in masonry terms, rubble refers to a wall made up of split or whole granite boulders, limestone or sandstone blocks of irregular size. The most common in North America is the wall of split boulders, "random laid" or "coursed." The former requires no explanation, but the latter will be recognized as following horizontal lines in the mortar joint. The line of mortar will rarely be continuous throughout the length of the barn, but the horizontality of the coursing will be the characteristic feature of the wall.

Either random or coursed, a rubble wall is a beautiful one in both colour and texture. The individual stones were originally granite boulders split by a well-aimed blow from the mason. Some, inelegantly called "nigger heads", would not split, and went into the wall as they were left by the glacier. In spite of their seeming ruggedness, these rubble walls are not structurally ideal. Originally round, the only flat face of the boulder is that toward the outside, and a round-bottomed, round-topped stone set in mortar has not the stability of a flat stone.

In various places including the province of Quebec, rubble walls are sometimes built in forms like concrete. The result is a fine looking wall with much exposed mortar on the face of the stone. It is not a method of building approved by urban codes.

Ashlar Ashlar is rare in barns. (See *quoin*.) It refers to stone which has been sawn on all four faces and laid on its "natural bed," or the way it was found in the quarry. Ashlar is the walling of the great buildings of antiquity like St. Peters in Rome. When seen today, the name is not justified, as "ashlar" is but veneer of four-inch to six-inch slabs set in a wall of tile or concrete.

Cobbles Where cobbles are found in a district, they are used with great effect on houses, barns and even churches. The effect is wholly one of texture, of the sun casting shadows on a thousand round stones, but structurally the cobbles contribute nothing to the stability of the wall, which is entirely dependant on the backing of brick or concrete.

a) In a scene that might be biblical at the time of Ruth, an Amish girl harrowing in Ontario.

b) A sheep-shed (worthy of a better name) in which the texture of the wall is matched on a smaller scale by that of the roof.

c

e

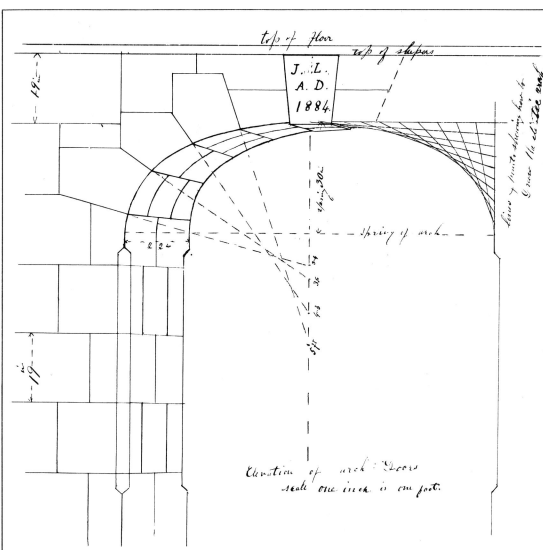

top of floor

top of stepers

J. W. L.
A. D.
1884.

Spring of arch

Elevation of arch : Doors
scale one inch in one foot.

d

f

c,d) The importance of manure in the farm economy in
1884 may be judged by the elegance of the arch and
the architect's very precise drawing for the mason.

e) It is rare to find a Dutch door to a granary—here over
the stable door in a well-built wall of flat stones.

f) A colourful rubble wall with ventilating embrasures.

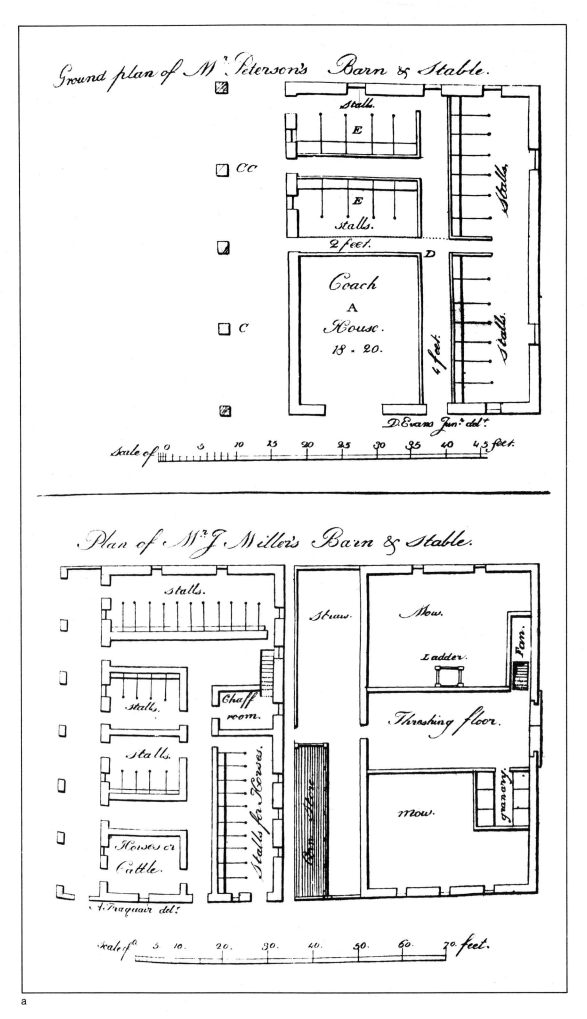

Ground plan of Mr. Peterson's Barn & Stable.

Stalls.

E

CC

E

stalls.

2 feet.

Stalls

D

Coach
A
House.
18 . 20.

4 feet.

Stalls

C

Stalls

D. Evans Junr. delt.

Scale of 0   5   10   15   20   25   30   35   40   45 feet.

Plan of Mr. J. Miller's Barn & Stable.

stalls.

Straw.

Mow.

Fan.

Ladder.

Chaff
room.

stalls.

Threshing floor.

sta lls.

Stalls for Horses.

Corn store

Granary.

Howses or
Cattle.

mow.

A. Traquair delt.

Scale of 0   5   10.   20.   30.   40.   50.   60.   70. feet.

a

Mortise A rectangular slot cut into one member to receive the tenon (usually at right angles) from another member-for strength, the slot was never wider than one-third the member.

Mow A part of the barn used for storing hay and sheaves of grain.

Pennsylvania Barn-Historic Plans Plans of a very convenient barn, coach-house and stable under one roof built on Mount Prospect, Bristol Road; and a substantial barn and stables in Chester County, Pennsylvania. The diagram of the Miller barn is the earliest known architectural plan of a two-storey Pennsylvania barn. Dr. James Mease writes of the Miller barn that "the whole barn is plastered, and there are venetian blinds to all the windows."[1] The reader may be confused by the proximity of the two plans of the Miller barn. The plan on the right is of the upper floor, which should be thought of as sitting over the cattle floor on the left. There is an overhang to the threshing floor, but it is supported on posts.

Piggery Housing for the hog population has improved greatly in the last decade or so, and isolated buildings like those on page 199 are rarely found. Since they did not lend themselves to contemporary thinking in terms of hygiene and the general welfare of the inhabitants, a more sterile, sunlit structure doubtless took their place.

Pin A dowel or trunnel (treenail) most often made from white ash, oak, or hickory, and used to secure mortise and tenon or half lap joint.

Plate The long horizontal timber which is the topmost member on the side frame of the barn, where it carries the heel of the rafters.

Purlin This is a heavy timber, usually square in section, running longitudinally under the rafters midway between plate and ridge. Its function is to take some of the strain off the rafters which support the load of the roof including snow. The purlin is upheld by posts at bay intervals and sometimes braced by diagonal timbers. Dimensions of 9″ x 9″ x 50'0″ for the purlin have been recorded and photographed in old barns.

a) Pennsylvania barn plans. See text above.

b

c

d

Quoin A rough dressed or ashlar-faced series of stones used to give strength, or the appearance of strength, to a wall. It would provide a random rubble wall with real stability, and it would be obligatory on a "stovewood" wall. In both cases the quoin would be used on corners, whether the corner was on a rectangular or a polygonal barn.

The quoin may present a simple vertical face like a pilaster, or a number of stones of alternating widths. In the latter case, the quoin gives the wall greater strength by reason of the interlocking stones.

Quoin on a brick wall would likely be purely decorative.

Rack Lifter A horse-driven mechanism situated in the beams over the drive or threshing floor. It lifted the loaded *hay rack* from the hay wagon to the necessary height where the hay was forked by hand into the mow.

Rafters Rafters are the important timbers in the framing of the barn that support the roof. They slope from the ridge to the plate at the foot, but on the way they get support from the purlin, a heavy transverse beam running the length of the barn. Spacing is generally at three-foot intervals, but in the Quebec barn, where the annual snow-fall and the roof boards are heavy, rafters themselves are heavy and separated by as much as five feet. They may be sawn, adzed, tapered, or just the limbs of trees shorn of their branches.

Ridge Piece or **Ridgepole** A horizontal timber against which the rafters butt and are supported at the apex of the roof.

Roofs Of the varieties of roof described here, the gabled and the hipped are by far the most common, and of more ancient lineage than the gambrel or the mansard. Other types occasionally encountered might be called-for want of better terms-gabled hip and hipped gable.
Gable The gable is the triangular upper part of the wall terminating the roof. It may be steep (French) or gentle in slope (Mediterranean). The carpenter's term for the latter is "one-third pitch".
Hip While the gable is a termination of the roof in a vertical plane (the wall), the hipped roof is formed in the roof itself and slopes from the ridge to the eaves at the same pitch as the main roof. It may be steep or one-third pitch,

b) The purlin supporting the rafters, and itself supported by the top beam via the angled purlin post. The whole is securely braced in both planes.

c) In early barns, many hewn rafters were joined by a half-lap and pinned.

d) In this roof of ridge-piece construction, the braced king posts take the load.

Some roof types

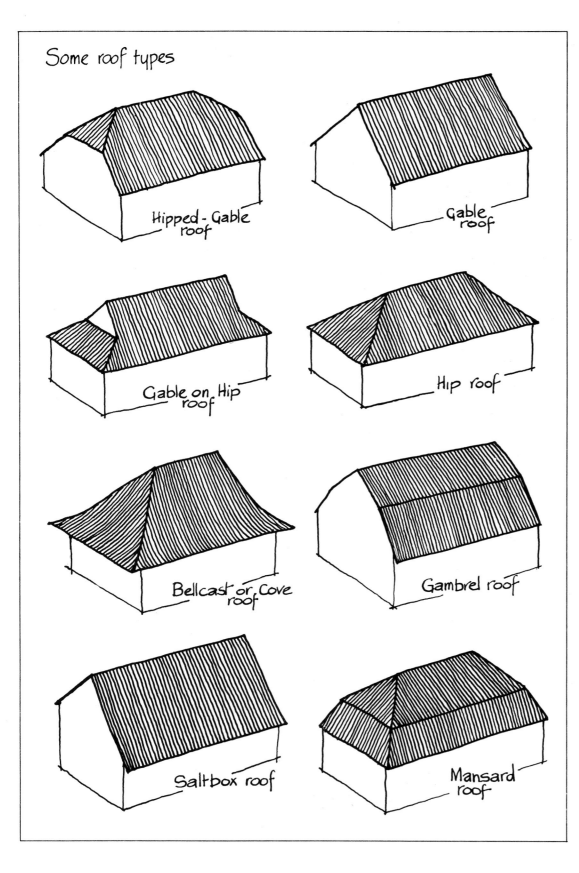

Hipped-Gable roof

Gable roof

Gable on Hip roof

Hip roof

Bellcast or Cove roof

Gambrel roof

Saltbox roof

Mansard roof

or somewhere in between. This roof is commonly known as "cottage."

Gambrel The gambrel roof, like the gable, ends in a vertical wall. But, unlike the gable, its section is an acute angle, rising steeply from the eaves, and then obtuse to the ridge. It has the great advantage of being roomier than the gable roof, has greater cubic capacity, and the mow floor is usable right up to the steeply sloping wall. The gambrel appeared in the second half of the nineteenth century as an answer to the need for greater storage space for hay or sheaves, but its origin is obscure. Eric Sloane suggests that its prototype may be the gambrel used by the butcher for the hanging of a carcase; and, in that case, the addition of the steeper slope on each side has to be imagined.

Mansard The mansard roof was named after the distinguished seventeenth-century French architect François Mansard, the designer of the Church of Val-de-Grâce and the Hôtel des Invalides. It has all the qualities of the gambrel but differs in that it terminates in a "hip" and not in a wall.

Collar-Beam Roof A roof in which the rafters are tied together halfway up by a tying piece called a collar.

Couple Roof A roof with no collar-beam or purlins, used for shorter spans.

Close-Boarded Roof A roof that is covered with boards touching each other; these are also the nailing support for the shingles.

Double Roof A roof where the rafters are supported on purlins which in turn are supported by trusses or other supports.

Pitch The term used to describe the angle of a roof. Pitch may be slight, as in some English barns, or steep, as in French Canadian ones. The cedar shingle roof requires a slope sufficient to shed water or snow and not to contain it, whereas a slate roof may be slight in pitch, steep, or even, with care, flat. What is true of the slate roof is, of course, true for copper, galvanized iron, or aluminum.

Above these practical considerations is the powerful influence of tradition. Renaissance architecture in England was profoundly affected by Italy, and the three-bay barn in Ontario reflects this influence, though far from home, in a roof of easy Mediterranean pitch. Although influenced by the same great movement in the arts, the French could not resist the force of the traditional roof of the Middle Ages, which was steep. It remains steep to this day in the province of Quebec.

a

Saltbox A term of unknown origin used to describe a house or barn in which the main roof is extended without a break to include accommodation at the rear. Usually of frame construction, saltbox barns were built throughout the nineteenth century. Many have all the appearance of a saltbox, but owe their silhouette to the addition of a lean-to which may have been needed for cattle, implements, or other purposes. It has been said that in the true saltbox the main wall faced south and the rear low wall north.

Sill The large foundation timber or timbers horizontally placed on a stone foundation, but sometimes on cedar or other wooden posts.

Silo Adding greatly to one's enjoyment of the barn are those minor buildings such as the silo, dairy, smoke house and the corn crib. Like the barn, they can be looked at in terms of form, function and material, and where all, or a majority of them, are contemporary with the barn, one gets that same feeling of homogeneity that has been observed in the snake fence and the dry enclosing walls.

Old dictionaries describe the silo "as a pit or tight structure in which green crops are pressed and kept for fodder undergoing fermentation." An article dated 1885 states that the system of storing green fodder is of Hungarian origin, introduced in 1875 to British farmers in an article by a Professor Wrightson in the *Journal* of the Royal Agricultural Society. At that time, the system consisted of cramming the green fodder tightly into deep wide trenches-wetness having the merit, it was claimed of easy packing and of preservation. In the same article, France is said to have practised the system for several years and given it the title *ensilage* meaning literally a pit or trench. A portion of the ensilage was taken out each day for use the next day, as after twenty-four hours' exposure "it will have passed the proper limit of fermentation."[2]

On an ordinary farm of 100 acres, certainly the smallest unit today, a silo 18 feet in diameter and 18 feet high will hold about 100 tons of corn silage, and one acre is capable of producing 12 tons.

The first silo as an upright structure is said to have been built in 1873 by Fred Hatch in McHenry County, Illinois.[3] Without a date on a barn or a document telling of its building, its age is difficult to determine and never with absolute precision. Much more difficult is an

a) The common wood silo, with a picturesque top.
Location: near Lindsay, Ontario.

b) A massive stone silo.
Location: near Clifford, Ontario.

b

estimation of the age of a silo. Did Mr. Hatch's successors build their silos of wood, stone or brick? One would guess from the primitive, rugged appearance of these structures that the square silo with heavy timber framing outranks all others in longevity.

An interesting development, though short-lived, was the placing of the silo inside the barn. In such a position, dramatic solutions were achieved both inside and outside the barn as the silo rose above the roof. In its most architectural form it is seen in the Shaker barn at Hancock and *"la ferme des enfants"* in Quebec, and less subtly in the stone barn outside Edmonton, Alberta.

The external square silo attached to the barn can be a very handsome structure, whether the framing is exposed or covered by vertical planking as it is seen in Vermont. In Ontario, it appears as a primitive structure, seemingly unfinished and waiting its outer covering of boards or shingles. It is, however, wherever found, perfectly plumb. The same cannot be said of the most common of all silos, those constructed of thin boards and bound at intervals with hoops of wire. These are rarely perpendicular, and lean at an angle away from the prevailing wind, or even of the previous wind. They do not represent rural architecture in its most substantial form, but more than other types of silo, they show an infinite variety of roof tops, from the cove to its opposite the dome. In this latter form, they were the forerunners of the great tile and concrete silos that are the latest product of agricultural technology and nearly always crowned by a dome. Only one suggestion has been made as to why or when silos were built in stone or brick. Eric Sloane is of the opinion that the late 1800's marked the time when charcoal making for iron foundries exhausted many American woodlots, and stone or brick were the only materials available. Whatever the reason, those that are left to us are often beautiful. They may glow in the sun in multicoloured brick, or suggest in weathered stone or cobble an age centuries before their inception on the farm. Even abandoned and topless, they have an irresistible charm, which they share with a silo of another material, the circular silo sheathed in silver-toned shingles.

Slick A large chisel worked with both hands for trimming joints on the barn frame.

a) A timber framed and wired silo with cupola. Location: near Naples, New York.

a

Stall Ancient writers recommended four feet for an ox in its stall and eight feet, though sometimes seven, for a yoke. The suggestion has been made that the persistence of the four-foot stall through more than two thousand years may account for the fact that the length of many barns is divisible by four and most are an even number of feet. While that is mere speculation, it is true that timber scantlings are sold in even feet–10′, 12′, 14′, 16′, etc.

Stovewood Wall This is a good-looking wall, in which short lengths of birch or other wood in the round are laid in mortar. Birch is the most popular, and the ends are often tarred. The pieces are about sixteen inches long, and the result is a far from stable structure without a stone quoin or heavy vertical timbers on corners and at window and door openings. It is a cheap wall, and in seeing it one can imagine the co-operation in its building of an entire young family. With the nice white logs cut and their ends tarred, the children could pass the pieces to their elders who were mixing and laying the mortar.

The Tithe The payment of tithe had rather a grim origin. It all began when King Offa of Mercia, who was crowned in 755 A.D., gave one-tenth of all the products of his kingdom to the church in expiation for the death of his brother Ethelbert, whom he had murdered. It was not until 1200 A.D. that tithes were ordered to be paid in England to the particular parish in which they arose, and payment in kind persisted until 1836.

Like most taxes, the tithe was unpopular, and, frequently, with reason. We have the word of that most charitable of men, the blessed Sir Thomas More that "noblemen and gentlemen, yea, and certain abbots, holy men God wot, not contenting themselves with the yearly revenues and profit that were wont to grow to their forefathers and predecessors of their lands...leave no ground for tilling: they throw down houses, they pluck down towns [villages] and leave nothing standing but only the church to make it only a sheep cote."[1] That sorry state of affairs, one hopes, was not too common, but as Sir Thomas wrote, the dissolution of the monasteries was already taking place. It is fortunate that records exist of how the tithe "operated," and, again, how those who paid were rewarded. "When the corn was in stoock or shoch as it was sometimes called,

b, c) The cow stalls in the byre and the horse stalls in the stable.
Location: near Milton, Ontario.

233

a

the parson's man went around and stuck a green bough in every tenth stook. Presently, the parson's wain rumbled along and took away every stook that had a bough in it. In a parish with 5,000 acres, and the corn stood thick in 1800 when corn was dear because of the Napoleonic wars, the Vicar of Bilbury in Gloucestershire cleared 1,200."[5]

His treatment of the harvesters to whom he was so considerably indebted is not recorded, but if Parson James Woodford's treatment was typical, there was no feeling of ill will. On September 14, 1776, he wrote in his diary: "very busy all day with my barley, did not dine till five in the afternoon. My harvest men dined here today and gave them some beef and plumb [sic] pudding and as much liquor as they would drink. This evening finished my harvest and all carried into the Barn-8 acres." And again in December: "...by frolic for my people to pay tithe to me this day. I gave them a good dinner, surloin of beef roasted and plumb pudding in plenty.[6]

Tongue In common use in flooring and wall boarding are the terms "T and G," or "T and G and V-jointed," where a projection or tongue on one board fits into a groove on the next. This produces a flush surface which may be V-jointed.

The tongue by itself may be seen in the framing of the Dutch barn-a timber passing through the post and protruding as a "tongue," usually with curved end.

Ventilation Ventilation, which is so essential to the health of hay or other crops in the barn, takes so many forms that they are best listed.

1. At its most primitive, it is seen in the log barn merely as unchinked cracks caused by shrinkage between the timbers. It must be confessed that in many old frame or clapboarded barns, which in a hundred and more years have never seen a coat of paint, light streams in between the boards and the wind whistles. Ventilation without cost or mechanical aids is thorough.

2. Some quite elegant barns have louvered panels on bay centres.

3. The cupola, which is described elsewhere, serves both as lantern and ventilator, and is ideally placed on the ridge for such a purpose.

4. The "marten holes" in the gable ends of the Dutch barns of New York State provide a draft and easy access for the martens.

a) A very interesting log wall in which the logs lie comfortably on each other, tapering from different ends in alternate courses. What might be missed is that the logs are chinked with mortar only part way up as a protection against the wind for the cows inside. There is no chinking above, as ventilation was needed for the hay.

b

c

5. Because of the nature of the crop, ventilation in tobacco barns in the United States is carefully planned and, in the most notable examples, involves cutting out a panel in a board and batten wall. The panel is narrow, extending to the full height of the wall, hinged at the top, and adjustable at the base. Alternatively, it may swivel. Several of these give great interest to a wall, altogether apart from their effectiveness as ventilators.

6. Some quite beautiful barns and stables have double hung windows. It is doubtful that they were ever operated as ventilators and became effective only when, by accident or design, the panes were broken.

7. Where ventilation was desirable in the masonry wall, whether of stone or of brick, the builder had fewer options. Universal in its usage was the "slit," or embrasure-a whole series of them at different levels in the wall. Occasionally, the reveals to the embrasure are flaired on the inside like their prototypes in fortified buildings of the Middle Ages, but usually for economy of labour they are not.

8. Very rare indeed is the deliberate planning of ventilation by means of a flue in the thickness of the wall. The example illustrated, near Eramosa, Ontario, ventilates the stable, and may be unique.

9. In brickwork, the last word in ventilation is said in Pennsylvania. By the simple device of omitting bricks, superb examples of the bricklayer's craft were displayed on gable ends, and a through draft was guaranteed.

b) A windmill near Mildmay, Ontario.

c) A windmill near St. Raphael, Bellechaisse County, Quebec.

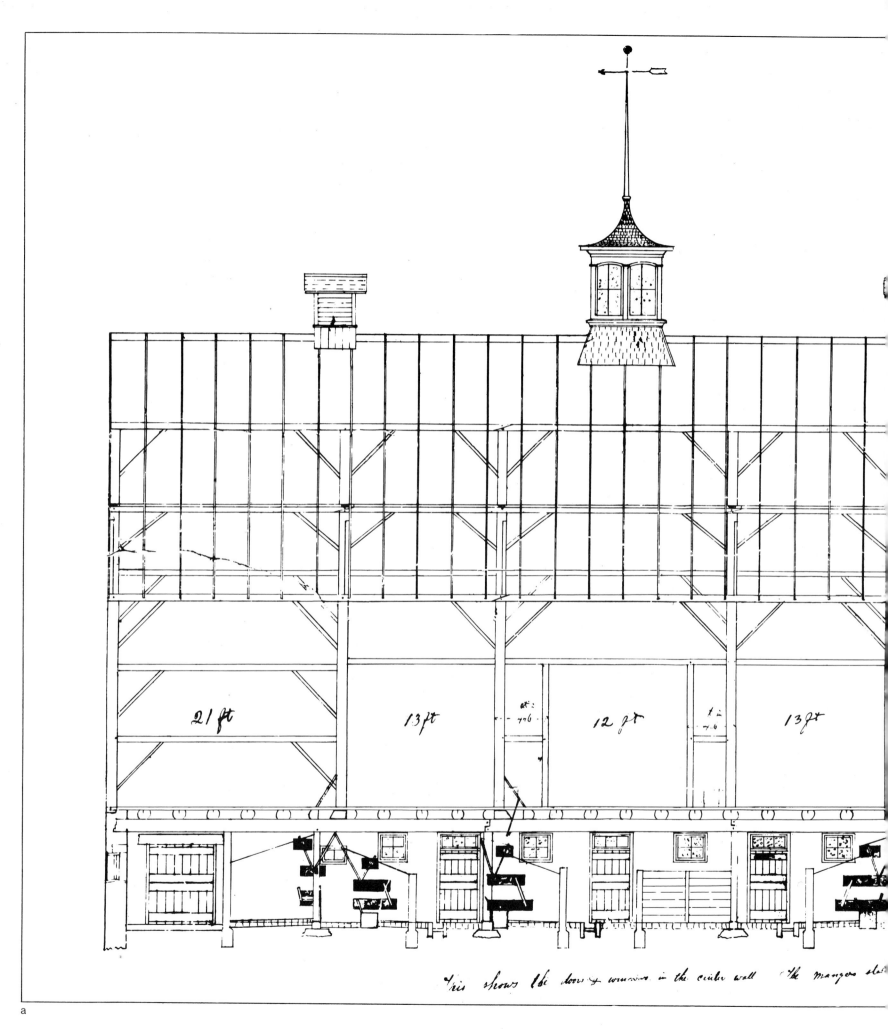

21 ft   13 ft   at : — 7·6   12 ft   t : 7·6   13 ft

This shows the doors & windows in the center wall   the mangers sh...

a

236

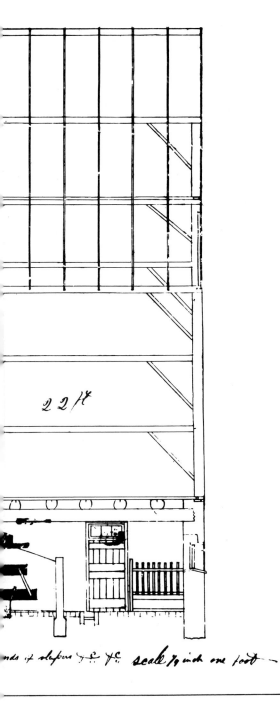

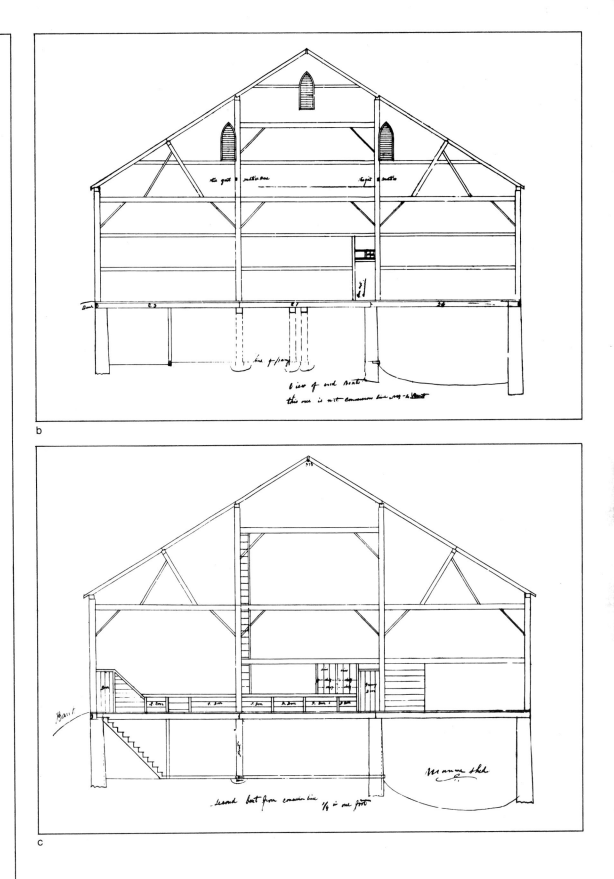

b

c

a-c) As Mr Lacy says in his Foreword, our old barns were "designed by men who didn't know they were designers." They knew intuitively the kind of structure that was needed. Rare in the eighteenth or nineteenth century were barns for which an architect provided drawings and specifications. We have such material, the specification in longhand signed "Thos Ruddell, Arc^{k}" for a barn in Ontario in the 1880's. He would be the envy of all modern architects if they could end their specifications as he has–"As many things cannot be minutely mentioned, it is expected that any thing required to properly complete the job, shall be done as if it had been mentioned particularly."

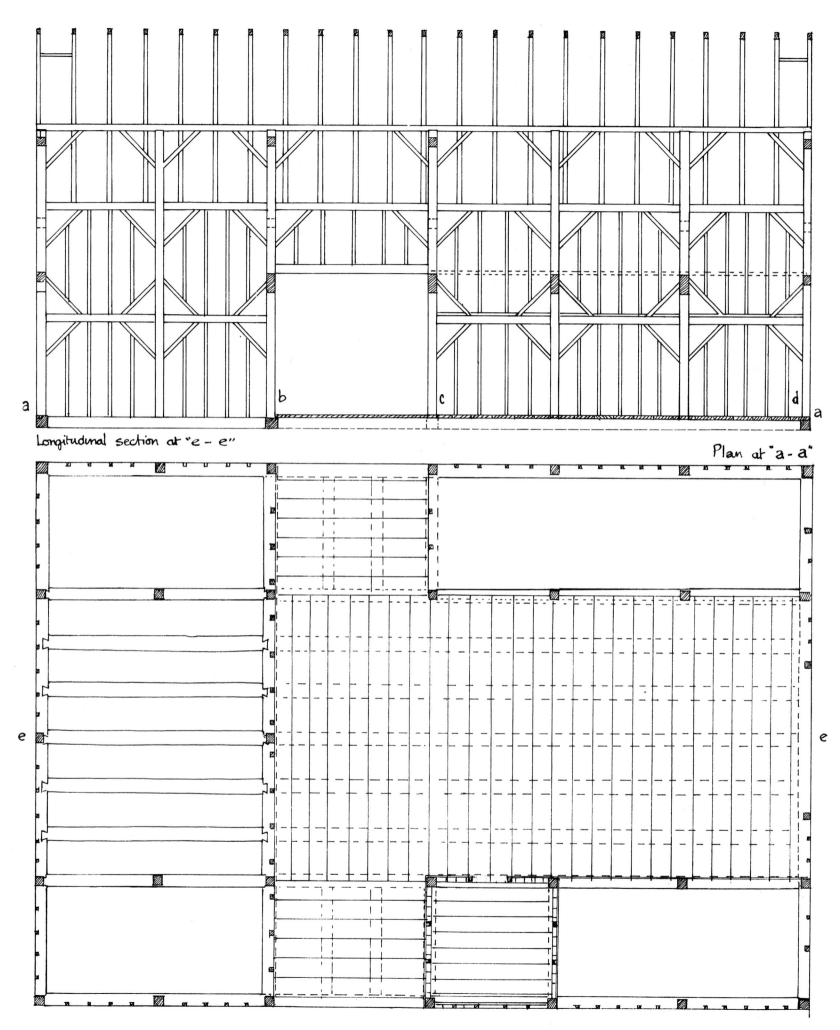

Longitudinal section at "e - e"

Plan at "a - a"

a   b   c   d   a

e   e

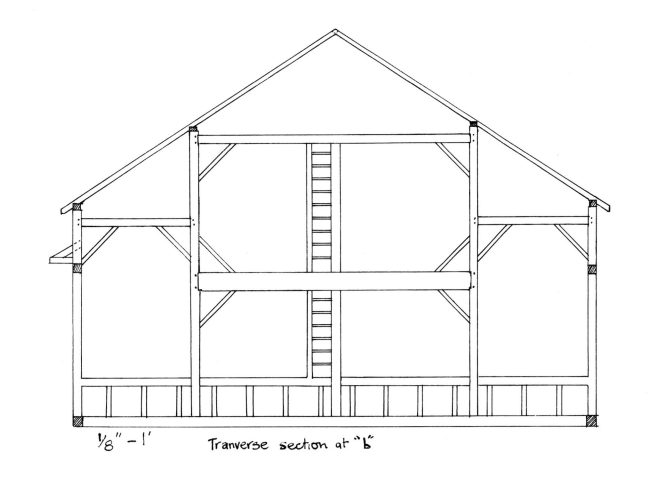

1/8" – 1'   Tranverse section at "b"

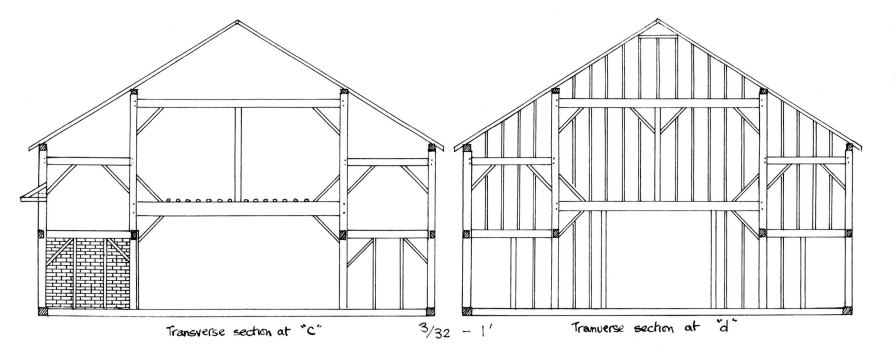

Transverse section at "c"   3/32 – 1'   Tranverse section at "d"

Framework diagram of the Seebold barn. Schoharie, New York.

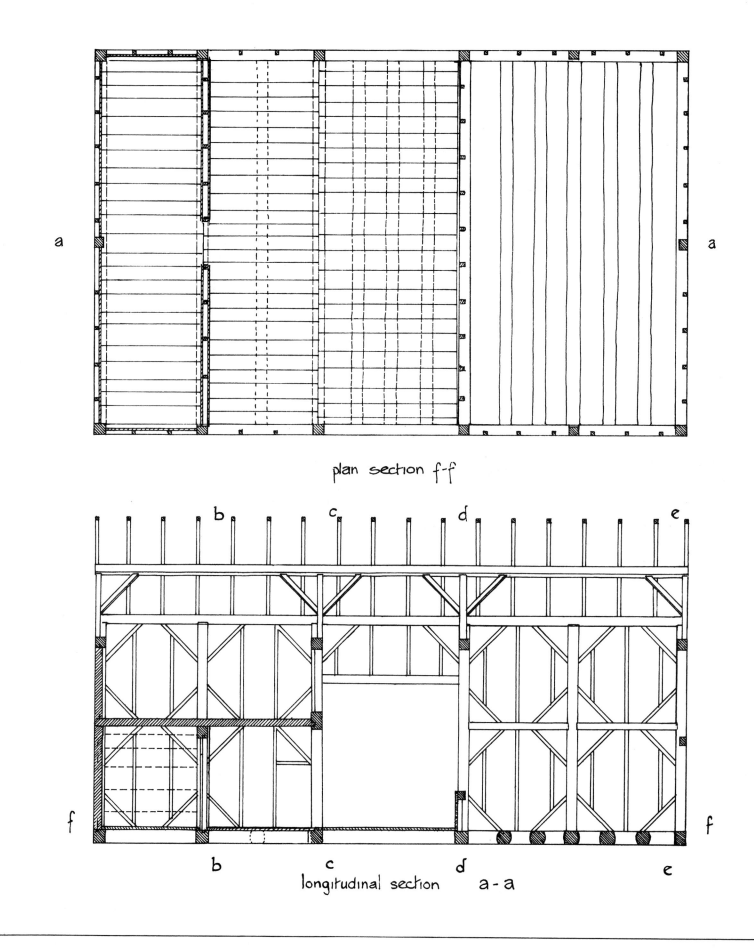

plan section f-f

longitudinal section a-a

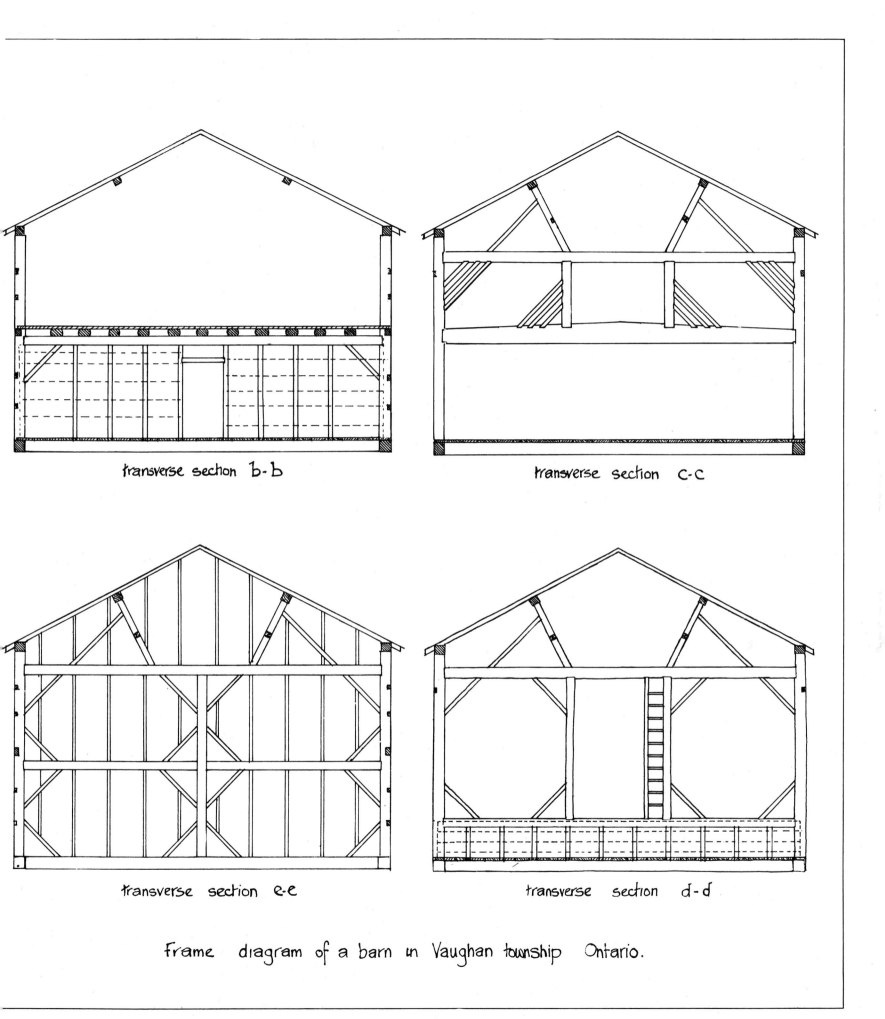

transverse section b-b

transverse section c-c

transverse section e-e

transverse section d-d

Frame diagram of a barn in Vaughan township Ontario.

241

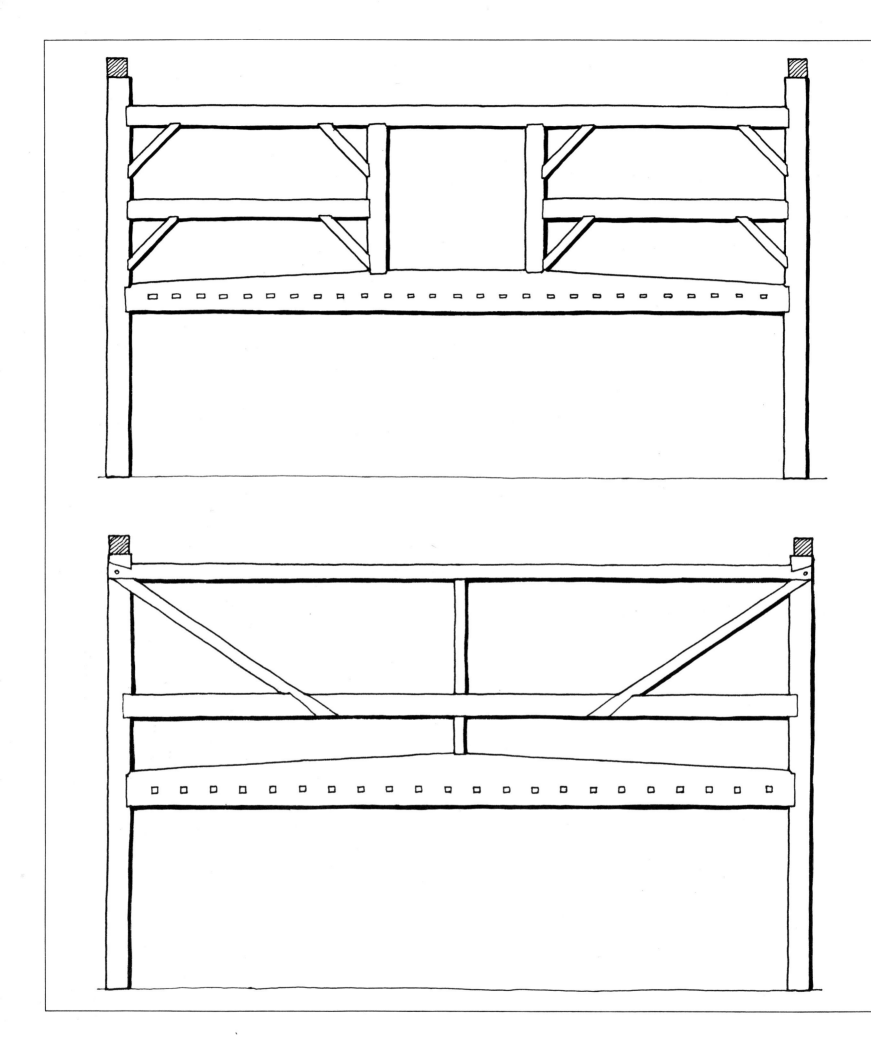

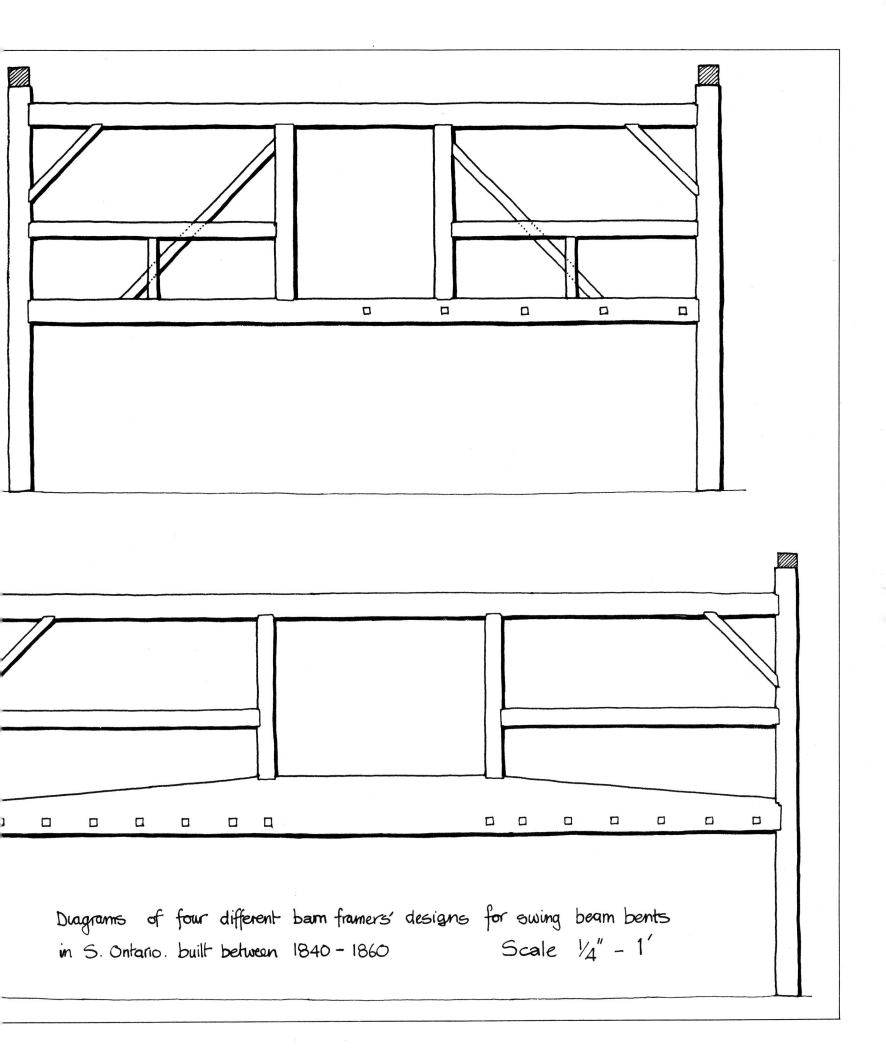

Diagrams of four different barn framers' designs for swing beam bents in S. Ontario. built between 1840 - 1860   Scale ¼" - 1'

Notes

INTRODUCTION

1. Olive Cook, *English Farm Houses and Cottages,* p. 8.

2. W. H. Graham, *The Tiger of Canada West* (Toronto: Clarke, Irwin, 1962), p. 68.

3. Samuel Thompson, *Reminiscences of a Canadian Pioneer,* p. 47.

4. W. H. Graham, *The Tiger of Canada West,* p. 69.

5. *Ibid.,* p. 70.

6. For example, by the United States Department of the Interior, the National Parks Service, and the Historic American Building Survey.

7. Frederick Klees, *Pennsylvania Dutch.* For readers not familiar with the two views, each vehemently held in Pennsylvania, it should be explained that Mr. Klees represents a group who insist on calling the German-speaking Mennonites and Amish, Dutch. The word, if a Canadian may be so bold as to express an opinion, would seem to have come from the German *Deutsch.* Settlers of Dutch origin settled on the banks of the Hudson River in New York State; though, to confuse the issue, many did settle in Pennsylvania.

8. The 1970 edition deals largely with management, building practice, etc., and not with history. "Although the need for the general barn declined with the advent of the tractor and electric service, one or more barns are still found on the majority of North American and European farms. Many have been adapted to other services."

9. Readers interested in shooting may like to know of another curious piece of information: "Barley corn, a unit of measure ⅓ of an inch–top of foresight on a rifle." (Oxford Dictionary.)

10. "In the village of Chysauster near Penzance in England, there is a row of eight stone houses of the first century B.C. that in plan are as rudimentary in terms of human comfort as anything built in prehistoric times. Each cottage consists of two apartments, a living room and a byre, each with its own small courtyard–a very strange anachronism, but one, we are told, that persisted elsewhere in England right up to modern times." (Martin S. Briggs, *The English Farmhouse,* p. 15.)

11. W. H. Graham, *The Tiger of Canada West,* p. 150.

12. Eric Sloane, *An Age of Barns* (New York: Funk & Wagnalls, 1967).

13. John Fitchen, *The New World Dutch Barn* (Syracuse: Syracuse University Press, 1968), and Alfred Shoemaker (ed.), *The Pennsylvania Barn* (Lancaster, Pennsylvania: Franklin Dutch Folklore Center, 1955).

14. R. L. Séguin, *Les Granges du Québec* (Ottawa: Musée National du Canada, 1963).

THE DUTCH BARN

1. The Basilican plan will also be seen, in many instances, in the Pennsylvania barn.

2. M. E. Christie [M. E. Seebohm], *Evolution of the English Farm* (London: Allen & Unwin, 1927), p. 80.

3. The term dates from Saxon times. The "goodman" had to cross the threshing floor (called *therscold*) to get to his living quarters, and the word has survived in the entrance step to a house.

4. Sidney O. Addy, *Evolution of the English House,* p. 104.

5. William Harrison, *England,* quoted in Addy, p. 95.

6. *Ibid.,* p. 96. Near Peterborough, Ontario, there is a stable attached to a large barn, and the story seems well authenticated that, in the 1860's when the barn was built, the well-lit handsome space over the horse stalls served as a dormitory for stable-men. For the only example in North America of the house-barn connection, see the chapter on the connected barn.

7. John Fitchen, *The New World Dutch Barn,* p. 19.

8. *Ibid.*

THE ENGLISH BARN

1. *Communications of the Board of Agriculture* (London: 1797).

2. The term "two-bay barn" may have originated in the brick barn in England, but to be strictly correct the North American two-bay barn in timber consists of three or more bays formed by posts separating areas for livestock and/or storage from the threshing floor.

3. Peter M. Ennals, "The Development of Barn Types in South Eastern Ontario during the Nineteenth Century." (Unpublished thesis.)

4. Anthony Garvan, in *Architecture and Town Planning in Colonial Connecticut.*

5. Harold R. Shurtleff, *The Log Cabin Myth,* (Cambridge: Harvard University Press, 1939), p. 37.

6. *Ibid.,* p. 65.

7. *Ibid.,* p. 3.

8. Henry Glassie, "The English or Connecticut Barn" in *Pennsylvania Folklife,* vol. 15, no. 2, p. 11. See also in appendix to this volume the use of plank in old Quebec.

9. Henry Glassie, "The Old Barns of Appalachia" in *Mountain Life and Work,* 1965.

THE PENNSYLVANIA BARN

1. T. J. Wertenbaker, *The Founding of American Civilization: The Middle Colonies* (New York: Cooper Square Publishers), p. 321.

2. *Ibid.,* p. 322.

3. *Ibid.,* p. 323.

4. *Ibid.*

5. *Ibid.,* p. 63.

6. E. O'Callaghan, *History of New Netherland,* quoted in Wertenbaker, p. 62.

7. John K. Heyl, in his introduction to C. H. Dornbusch, *The Pennsylvania German Barn.*

8. See Alfred Shoemaker, *The Pennsylvania Barn,* p. 27. The supporting columns are typical of the forebay in the Chester, Delaware County area.

9. In *The New World Dutch Barn,* Professor Fitchen refers to the pentice over the doors on the Dutch barn. He argues that its purpose was not so much the protection of the doors as the threshold or door sill. The same would apply in the Pennsylvania barn where, as was sometimes the case, a pentice covered the wagon doors.

10. Alfred Shoemaker, *The Pennsylvania Barn,* p. 38.

11. *Ibid.,* Percentages for stone barns in 1798 are given on page 37, frame on page 38, and brick on page 87.

12. *Ibid.,* p. 38.

13. See the chapter on the English barn.

14. J. William Stair, "Brick End Decorations" in *Pennsylvania Folklife,* vol. 15A, p. 23.

15. *Ibid.*

THE CONNECTED BARN

1. "Edible seeds of leguminous plants–e.g. lentils, peas, etc." (Oxford dictionary.)

2. R. L. Séguin, *Les Granges du Quebec,* p. 18.

3. *Ibid.,* p. 23.

4. *Ibid.,* p. 26.

5. *Ibid.,* p. 27.

6. Another authority whom it is a pleasure and a duty to acknowledge is M. Pierre Deffontaines for his *L'Homme et l'hiver au Canada* (Quebec: Les Presses de l'Université de Laval, 1957).

7. Dr. Wilbur Zelinsky made a special study of the connected barns in New England, and found that out of 4,376 barns seen in six states, 897 or twenty per cent of them were connected. Writing in 1958, he was able to say: "More frequently, the house and barn are contiguous and share the full extent of one wall. Even more commonly the two meet along only part of a wall–en echelon. In both cases there is usually a door opening from the house directly into the barn." (Wilbur Zelinsky, "The New England Connected Barn," in *American Geographical Review,* 1958.)

8. *Ibid.,* quoting R. R. Walcott, "Husbandry in Colonial New England," an article in *New England Quarterly.* vol. 9, 1936, p. 233.

9. Herbert Wheaton Congdon, *Old Vermont Houses* (New York: Alfred A. Knopf, 1946), p. 73.

CIRCULAR AND POLYGONAL BARNS

1. John I. Rempel, *Building in Wood* (Toronto: University of Toronto Press, 1967), p. 174.

2. *Ibid.*

3. The province of Quebec is rich in circular and many-sided barns, all of them of the late nineteenth century and earlier. Writing in *Vermont Life* in the summer of 1971, Stephen Whitney was of the opinion that, up until 1914, "two dozen round barns may have been erected here. Twelve still stand."

4. Eric Sloane, *An Age of Barns,* p. 52.

5. From *The Round Stone Barn: a short history for the Friends of Hancock Shaker Village on the occasion of the opening of the restored barn.*

THE DECORATIVE ARTS

1. Mary Mix Foley, "The American Barn," *Architectural Forum,* August 1951, p. 170.

2. Earl F. Robaker, "Butter Moulds" in *The Dutchman,* June 1954, pp. 6–8.

3. Preston A. Barba, in "Pennsylvania German Tombstones, a Study in Folk Art." In his *Book of Signs,* published first in Germany, Rudolph Koch writes that the four-pointed star "is a phenomenon carrying a grave and solemn warning; the five leaves an impression of cheer and happiness, but the six bears the same urgent message as the four." This he claims is the true star and satisfies most nearly the general conception of a star.

4. Oxford Dictionary.

5. Patricia Mullen, *The Plain People* (Witmer, Penn.: Applied Arts, 1960), p. 51.

6. Dr. John J. Stoudt, in *Pennsylvania Folk Art* (Cranbury, N. J.: A. S. Barnes, 1948).

7. It has been suggested that the presence of a six-pointed star as a warning or a bearer of good luck may have appealed to fire insurance companies. Miss Lila Lerch (in the Reading *Times,* 1949) has shown that before 1800 a six-pointer was used as a fire mark by the Insurance Company of North America, and the Sun Fire Office required insured persons to mount its Sun Mark on their property.

8. Walter Boyer, ed., *Epis Fuum de Mahadunky* (Witner, Penn.: Applied Arts, 1948).

9. The stone is the property of Yosef Drenters at the Rockwood Academy which he has made his home. The Academy was a school for boys built in 1853 and had such pupils as Adam (later Sir Adam) Beck and James Hill who became well known in the United States in the railway wars which he waged with Gould, Morgan, and others of his time. He was born in Rockwood where his parents kept the inn.

THRESHING AND WINNOWING

1. Deut. 25:4.

2. Jahn's *Biblical Archaeology* (1827), p. 72.

3. Mabel Elizabeth Christie [M. E. Seebohm], *The Evolution of the English Farm,* p. 91.

4. *Ibid.,* p. 66.

5. *Ibid.,* quoting Martin, *Description of the Western Isles of Scotland.*

6. The problem of drying the grain continued into the nineteenth century, as can be seen in this advertisement from *The British American Cultivator:* "REVOLVING DRYING KILN. The Subscriber begs to inform the Millers, Merchants, and the Public generally, that he has, at considerable labor and expense, invented and completed a Machine for DRYING Wheat, Oats, Barley, Indian Corn, or any other Grain necessary to be dried before being manufactured: and he assures them, that it is the cheapest and most expeditious mode of Kiln Drying Grain now in use. This Machine will dry from thirty to sixty bushels of grain per hour in a most perfect manner. It is so constructed, that the grain passes through the machine, from thence to the rolling screen, where it is cooled, in a fit state for manufacturing. This machine requires very little power to keep it in motion, and may be driven by a small strap from any wheel in the mill. A quarter of a cord of hardwood will produce heat sufficient for drying a thousand bushels of grain.

"The Subscriber begs to inform the public, that he has obtained a Patent for his Machine, which extends throughout the United Province of Canada, and that he is prepared to manufacture the above Machines to order, or dispose of the right to persons desirous of manufacturing or using the same.

"Any further information on the subject may be had, by addressing the Subscriber. All communications (post-paid) will be immediately replied to.
HIRAM BIGELOW,
Tecumseth, Bond Head P.O.
February 15th, 1844."

7. Olive Cook and Edwin Smith, in *English Farm Houses and Cottages.*

8. "Because the 'horsey elite' of Toronto demanded clean bundled straw for bedding, an elderly Englishman, Mr. William Westland was hired to produce it by flailing. It is said that 200-300 bushels were done this way in the winter months, and his activities continued up until the end of the First Great War." (From a conversation with Mr. Clark Young of Unionville, Ontario.)

9. For this and much other information on threshing, see *Encyclopedia Britannica,* 11th edition, vol. 26, p. 887.

10. Ruth 2, 17.

11. See note 18.

12. Jared Van Wagenen, Jr., *The Golden Age of Homespun,* p. 240.

13. *Ibid.,* p. 242.

14. *Ibid.,* p. 240.

15. *Ibid.,* p. 242.

16. Dan. 2:35.

17. John S. McDonald, *Pioneering Near Ripley,* p. 258.

18. *M.E.S.* p. 311.

19. Matt, 3:12.

20. Van Wagenen, Jr., *The Golden Age of Homespun,* p. 240.

21. *Ibid.*

22. *Ibid.*

23. Christie [Seebohm], *The Evolution of the English Farm,* p. 67.

24. *Ibid.,* p. 175, and drawing of windmill from the Luttrell Psalter.

OMNIUM GATHERUM

1. Dr. James Mease, in his *Domestic Encyclopedia* (Philadelphia, 1804).

2. J. P. Sheldon, *Dairy Farming* (London: Cassell, 1885).

3. Eric Sloane, *An Age of Barns,* p. 62.

4. Martin S. Briggs, *The English Farm House* (London: Batsford, 1953), p. 41.

5. E. R. Yanham, "Britain's Ancient Tithe Barns" in *Family Herald and Weekly Star,* July 9, 1941.

6. Martin S. Briggs, *The English Farm House,* p. 194.

Bibliography

Addy, Sidney Oldall. *Evolution of the English House.* Revised and enlarged from the author's notes by John Summerson. London: Allen & Unwin, 1933.

Board of Agriculture [of England]. *Communications of the Board of Agriculture.* London, 1797.

The American Agriculturalist. Vol. 23. New York: Orange Judd Company, 1874.

B. T. Barn Book. Nos. 3, 39. Fergus, Ont.: Beatty Bros., n.d.

Barn Plans and Outbuildings. New York: Orange Judd Company, 1897.

Blake, V. B. "Schoharie Barns." Memorandum in the research library of Upper Canada Village, Morrisburg, Ont. Typescript.

Boyle, David, ed. *The Township of Scarborough, 1796–1896.* Toronto: William Briggs, 1896.

Briggs, Martin Shaw. *The English Farm House.* London: Batsford, 1953.

Christie, Mabel Elizabeth [M. E. Seebohm]. *The Evolution of the English Farm.* London: Allen & Unwin, 1927.

Congdon, H. W. *Old Vermont Houses.* New York: Alfred A. Knopf, 1946.

Cook, Olive, and Smith, Edwin. *English Farm Houses and Cottages.* London: Thames and Hudson, 1954.

Deffontaines, Pierre. *L'homme et l'hiver au Canada.* Paris: Gallimard, 1957.

Denison, Merrill. *Harvest Triumphant.* Toronto: McClelland and Stewart, 1948.

Dickerman, Charles W. *The Farmer's Book.* Philadelphia: Ziegler, McCurdy and Co., 1869.

Dodds, Eugene. *The Round Stone Barn: a short history for the Friends of Hancock Shaker Village on the occasion of the opening of the restored barn.* Shaker Community, Inc., 1968. Brochure.

Elmore, Reaman G. *The Trail of the Black Walnut.* Toronto: McClelland and Stewart, 1957.

Ennals, Peter M. "The Development of Farm Barn Types in Southern Ontario during the Nineteenth Century." Master's thesis, University of Toronto, 1968.

Fitchen, John. *The New World Dutch Barn.* Syracuse: Syracuse University Press, 1968.

Foley, Mary Mix. "The American Barn." *Architectural Forum,* August 1951.

Forrester, Harry. *The Timber-Framed Houses of Essex.* Chelmsford: Tindal Press, 1959.

Garvan, Anthony. *Architecture and Town Planning in Colonial Connecticut.* New Haven: Yale University Press, 1951.

Gauthier, Joseph-Stany. *Les Maisons Paysannes des Vieilles Provinces de France.* Paris: Éditions Charles Massin et Cie.

Glassie, Henry. *Pattern in the Material Folk Culture of the Eastern United States.* Philadelphia: University of Pennsylvania Press, 1969.

Harvey, Nigel. *A History of Farm Buildings in England and Wales.* Newton Abbot: David & Charles, 1970.

Hedrick, Ulysses Prentice. *A History of Agriculture in the State of New York.* New York: Hill and Wang, 1966.

Hewett, Cecil Alec. *The Development of Carpentry, 1200–1700.* Newton Abbott: David & Charles, 1969.

Horn, Walter, and Born, Ernest. *The Barns of the Abbey of Beaulieu at Its Granges of Great Coxwell and Beaulieu St. Leonards.* Berkeley: University of California Press, and London: Cambridge University Press, 1965.

Innocent, C. F. *The Development of English Building Construction.* Cambridge: Cambridge University Press, 1916.

Jans, Jan, and Van der Loeff, M. J. *Landelijke Bouwkunst in Oost-Nederland.* Enschede: M. J. Van der Loeff, 1969.

Kimball, Sidney Fiske. *Domestic Architecture of the American Colonies and the Early Republic.* New York: Scribner's, 1922.

Klees, Frederick, *Pennsylvania Dutch.* New York: Macmillan, 1950.

Loewe, Ludwig. *Schlesische Holzbauten.* Dusseldorf: Werner-Verlag, 1969.

McDonald, John S. *Pioneering Near Ripley.* Edited by W. L. Smith. Toronto: George N. Morang, 1923.

Pennsylvania Dutch Folklore Centre. *The Dutchman.* Various issues.

Pennsylvania Folklife. Various issues.

Rempel, John I. *Building in Wood.* Toronto: University of Toronto Press, 1967.

Ritchie, Thomas. *Canada Builds.* Toronto: University of Toronto Press, 1967.

Rudofsky, Bernard. *Architecture Without Architects.* New York: Museum of Modern Art, 1962.

Séguin, Robert Lionel. *Les Granges du Québec du 17e au 19e Siècle.* Ottawa: Musée National du Canada, 1963.

Shoemaker, Alfred L. *The Pennsylvania Barn.* Lancaster, Pennsylvania: Franklin Dutch Folklore Center, 1955.

Singer, Charles, Holmgard, E. J., and Hall, A. R. *History of Technology.* Vol. 1. London: Oxford University Press, 1954.

Sloane, Eric. *An Age of Barns.* New York: Funk & Wagnalls, 1967.

Smith, W. L. *The Pioneers of Old Ontario.* Toronto: George N. Morang, 1923.

Stotz, Charles Morse. *The Architectural Heritage of Early Western Pennsylvania.* Pittsburgh: University of Pittsburgh Press, 1966.

Thompson, Samuel, *Reminiscences of a Canadian Pioneer.* Toronto: Hunter Rose, 1884.

Van Wagenen, Jr., Jared. *The Golden Age of Homespun.* Ithaca: Cornell University Press, 1953.

Vermont Life. Various issues.

Walton, James. *Early Timbered Buildings of the Huddersfield District.* Huddersfield: Tolson Memorial Museum, 1955.

Wertenbaker, Thomas Jefferson. *The Founding of American Civilization: The Middle Colonies.* New York: Scribner's, 1938.

Whitney, Stephen T. "Round Barns." *Vermont Life,* Summer 1971.

Wilson, John M. *The Farmer's Dictionary.* Edinburgh: A. Fullarton & Co., n.d.

Zelinsky, Wilbur. "The New England Connected Barn." *Geographical Review,* October 1958.

Acknowledgements

The authors wish to thank primarily the Canada Council whose generous grant made this book possible. "A study of the barn in North America" at that time (1968) was thought to be an odd project, and the action of the Council gave the authors encouragement to pursue a subject that had already been an absorbing interest for many years. Books in English dealing exclusively with the barn and its history do not exist, but much valuable information has been gained in works concerned with the evolution of the English house or farm, in which the barn played an important role. Sources for this essential material and other references were found in the Pontifical Institute of Medieval Studies, the University of Toronto Library, and the Central Library of Metropolitan Toronto. We are deeply indebted to these institutions, and wish to express our sincere thanks to Father D. Finlay, Mr. Robert Blackburn, and Mr. Henry Campbell, their respective chief librarians.

Of very great assistance in our study of the Dutch barn in New York State and its history in Europe has been Dr. C. Th. Kokke, who provided us with plans and photographs of historic barns now restored and on public view in the open air museum at Arnhem in the Netherlands, where he is Head of Documentations.

Our special thanks go to M. R.L. Séguin for permission to quote freely from his admirable book, *Les Granges du Quebec,* and to Miss Nora Dawson who undertook, on our behalf, the translation of a substantial part of it. This was no easy task, as it included architectural terms of the seventeenth and eighteenth centuries now no longer in use.

We are greatly indebted to Their Excellencies, the Spanish Ambassador to Canada, Señor Juan José Rovira, and the Canadian Ambassador to Spain, Mr. J. E. G. Hardy, to whose active interest we owe the illustrations of the little known granaries of Galicia which we found interesting in the age long history of threshing.

Mr. Budd Feheley holds a unique position in the origins of this book in that he brought together two people who for many years had a common enchantment with the barn, and wished to share their enjoyment with others— if possible through the publication of a book. Without the collaboration which he brought about, it would not have been written.

It is a pleasure to express our indebtedness to Pamela Witney for her patience with one or both authors over several years, but, particularly, we are obliged to her for making contact easy with farmers in Quebec through her familiarity with the French language.

To Paul Arthur we are indebted for help on arriving at an editorial concept as well as for the design of this book. In addition Paul Arthur + Associates generously provided their facilities during its conception and production. In this connection, particular mention should be made of the contributions made by Ken Rodmell and Dennis Allard.

We are deeply indebted to the director of Architecture and Environmental Arts for the National Endowment for the Arts in Washington D.C., Bill N. Lacy, who in spite of his many public and academic responsibilities has shown a continued interest in the progress of our research into the barn in North America, and has done us the honour of writing the foreword to the book.

Mr. Paul Newberry, Format, for photographic printing.

Most generous has been the contribution of friends and others who led us down profitable paths in our search for barns, or whose advice we sought on a variety of agricultural topics.

Mr. Arthur Allen
Mrs. Bernice Ball
Mr. Clark Blair

Mr. C. G. J. Bond
Mr. and Mrs. Neil Bryson
Mr. George Burrell
Mr. David Chestnutt
Mr. Ralph Daly
Mr. Will Davies
Mr. Eugene Dodds
Mr. Yosef Drenters
M. Jean-Claude Dupont
Mr. A. T. Galt Durnford
Mr. Sterling D. Emerson
Mr. and Mrs. Howard Engel
Mr. and Mrs. James Fergusson
Mrs. Keith Franklin
Miss Doris Garbe
Mr. W. H. Graham
Dr. Erika Hanstaengl
Mr. Douglas Hough
Mr. Dean Hughes
Miss Mary Imrie
Mrs. B. B. Jennings
Mr. W. L. Kidd
M. Luc Lacourcière
Mrs. Sybil Longworth
Mr. Alois Matanovic
Mr. David Mackay
Mr. Basil McLean
M. Paul-Louis Martin

Dr. N. B. Millet
Mr. Stephen A. Otto
Mr. and Mrs. Howard Pain
Mr. and Mrs. Robert Pearson
Public Archives of Canada
Mrs. J. C. Rathbone
Mr. Simeon Reesor
Mr. John I. Rempel
Dr. Gisland Ritz
Mr. William Roberts
Mr. Emil Scherrer
Mme M. Stoffel
Mr. and Mrs. Robert Struble
Mr. Morley Symes
Mr. and Mrs. Maurice Thomas
Dr. Evan Turner
Mr. Clarence Vander Veer
Mr. Beat von Arx
Mr. Allert Warner
Mr. Bruce Watson
Mr. J. Watson Webb, Jr.
Mr. Leonard Wertheimer
Mr. G. Everett Wilson
Dr. Fritz Winter
Mr. Ronald Woodall
Mr. and Mrs. W. H. Woods
Mr. Clark Young

Photos and drawings by Dudley Witney with the exception of the following:

10a)11b) National Film Board, Ottawa
14a)14b)15c) Public Archives of Canada
16a)17c) National Monuments Records, London
28a) reproduction of the painting courtesy of William Roberts and The Roberts Gallery.
29b) Alois Matanovic
30, 31) drawings done from memory by eight- and nine-year-old children at school in the village of Unionville, Ontario.
40a)40c)41d)41e)41f) C. Th. Kokke
46a)47b) Clarke Blair, Fonda, N.Y.
48a) Clarence Vander Veer
48b) Smith's Photo Service, Morrisburg, Ont.
50a) Howard Engel
50c) Isabelle Eaglesham
70a)71c)71d) John S. O'Donnell
77c) Mr. and Mrs. W. H. Woods
92b) Chester County Historical Society—Ned Goode, West Chester, Penn.
115a)115b) Ontario Department of Tourism and Information
126a)126d) Inventaire des Oeuvres d'Art de la Province de Québec

130c)130d)138a) Public Archives of Canada
138c) Inventaire des Oeuvres d'Art de la Province de Québec
139f) Public Archives of Canada
139g) Ronald Woodall, West Vancouver, B.C.
141d) Inventaire des Oeuvres d'Art de la Province de Québec
148a) Isabelle Eaglesham
148b) 149c) John I. Rempel
182a) painting of hexes by Alois Matanovic
195c) Folklore Archives, Laval University (Collection J. C. Dupont)
202a) Ray Webber
210a) Clarence Vander Veer
215)216)217)218)219) G. F. Hoy
220a) Clemens Kalischer, Stockbridge, Mass.
222a) Department of Archives, Province of Ontario
226a) Alois Matanovic
227c)227d) Mr. and Mrs. G. Atkins
233b)233c) Alois Matanovic
235b)235c) Office du Film de la Province de Québec
Endpapers courtesy Metropolitan Toronto Central Library.

Index